Merton:
Mystic at the Center
of America

Thomas M. King, S.J.

A Michael Glazier Book
THE LITURGICAL PRESS
Collegeville, Minnesota

A Michael Glazier Book published by The Liturgical Press

Cover design by Don Bruno
Woodcut by Robert McGovern

1   2   3   4   5   6   7   8   9

Library of Congress Cataloging-in-Publication Data

King, Thomas Mulvihill, 1929–
    Merton : mystic at the center of America / Thomas M. King.
       p.   cm. — (The way of the Christian mystics ; 14)
    "A Michael Glazier book."
    Includes bibliographical references.
    ISBN 0-8146-5014-7
    1. Merton, Thomas, 1915–1968.   I. Title. II. Series: Way of the
Christian mystics ; v. 14.
BX4705.M542K55 1992
271'.12502—dc20
                                        91-46925
                                           CIP

Contents

Introduction   v

Chapter 1   SELF
   The Writer and the Self   1
   The Paradox of Delivery   12
   A Philosophy of the Individual and the Person   24

Chapter 2   CONTEMPLATION
   Contemplation: Metaphysical, Natural and
      Supernatural   37
   The Mystic and the Intellect   52
   Contemplation in Art and Life   64

Chapter 3   FREEDOM
   The Prisoner of Selfishness   76
   Proud Structure, Humble Freedom   86
   Journey to Freedom   96

Chapter 4   OTHERS
   Solitude and Society   107
   Action and Contemplation   120
   The Social Thought of a Contemplative   129

Epilogue   141

Bibliography   147

Introduction

In 1941 Thomas Merton left New York to spend Holy Week at a Trappist monastery in Kentucky. It was after dark when he first stood before the heavy wooden door of the Abbey of Gethsemani; as it opened he was "overpowered" by a new and different world: "I stepped into the cloister as into an abyss."

Dazed by images of monastic life he began writing hasty impressions in his journal:

> This is the center of America.
> I had wondered what was holding the country together, what has been keeping the universe from cracking in pieces and falling apart. It is places like this monastery.

When Holy Week was over, he returned to his teaching job in upstate New York, but he could not forget the monastery bells and the choir of white-cowled monks. The following December he returned to the monastery door hoping to enter as a postulant.

The Trappist monastery of Gethsemani is among the rolling hills of Kentucky, South of Louisville and Bardstown. It was the furthest West that Merton had been—the closest he had come to America's "center." But there was more to it than geography. In Gethsemani Merton would write of mystical prayer in the American idiom and speak to America's heart as no other spiritual writer had done. It is true he had spent much time abroad, but his fresh and bouyant prose captured the American spirit in the heady days that followed World War II. He would tell of Americans talking of the World Series and the Rose Bowl and add: "If ever there was a land where silence made men nervous and prayer drove them crazy and penance scared them to death, it is America" (WS, 17). Yet these were the people whom he saw turning to contemplation.

While a student at Columbia University, Merton was involved in college journalism, and his prose would always carry some of the youthful excitement of college life: he would tell of feeling "goosebumps all over," "burning up with the desire of God," "a good time that was so insane and idiotic," and being "grabbed by God." By such writing he made mystical graces a part of the American scene. He would tell of thinking about sanctifying grace as a permanent quality of the soul while sitting behind the dirty boxed hedges at Child's restaurant on 111th Street in New York City (SSM, 211). He would consider Christ as Light from Light, true God from true God while husking corn in a Kentucky barnyard. His faith was alive and fully American. His story, *The Seven Storey Mountain,*[1] was filled with a wide-eyed wonder that captured the pulse of America as it wakened to its own identity in the years following World War II. A fresh American voice, dwelling along the "Wilderness Trail" of Kentucky, was writing of ancient monks in the wilderness of Egypt. When his autobiography became a best seller, publishers were amazed to find accounts of mystical prayer at the center of American letters.

Thomas Merton was not born in America but in Prades in southwestern France on January 31, 1915. His mother was American and his father from New Zealand. As Tom turned one he was brought to live near his mother's parents in Douglaston, Long Island, where a younger brother was born. Tom was six when his mother died, and he went traveling with his father to Cape Cod and Bermuda before he was placed in a school in France. After further schooling in England (Oakham and Cambridge), he returned to the United States to begin the spring semester at Columbia in 1935. There in the fall of 1938 he converted to Catholicism; then he wrote a master's thesis on the poet William Blake and began teaching at St. Bonaventure's College (now University) in upstate New York. All these events were shaping the author who would write almost

---

[1] *The Seven Storey Mountain* was the non-fiction #3 best seller of the year. First and second were a book on playing canasta and a book of comic photos of animals. It has now sold over 3½ million copies.

sixty books telling of a spiritual journey that finished only with a sudden and accidental death in Bangkok on December 10, 1968. Then U.S. troops and supplies were flying into nearby Vietnam, so a somewhat empty U.S. army bomber flew his body back from Thailand for burial in the small Trappist cemetery at Gethsemani—the center of America where he had lived for twenty-seven years.

The writings of Merton are highly diverse. His earliest writings were short stories and novels; these were followed by a collection of poems. He wrote histories, biographies, an autobiography and a play; he wrote journals, book reviews, letters and articles. His writings would consider monastic liturgy and racial justice, Shaker furniture and scholastic philosophy, mysticism and SAC bombers crossing the Kentucky sky. He knew he was part of us and knew he had something to tell us—even before he knew what it was. The voice of Merton would change with the years, but America and the Church in America were changing too. The confident nation that discovered its strength in World War II was discovering its weakness in Vietnam, but through it all the voice of Merton called the nation to a spiritual heritage it seemed to forget. Merton brought a tradition of timeless truth to the times in which he lived. He told of finding the Absolute, yet all the while he was making his way through the relativity of life, one day at a time. A mystic was writing of his dilemmas, and they turned out to be our own.

This is the complex man and complex material at the base of the present study. It tries to present a somewhat systematic account of the mysticism of Merton. Yet the author knows there is a basic difficulty in attempting a systematic study of Merton or any other mystic, for the language of the mystic is filled with paradox. Most mystics would limit the paradox to their central experience: they would tell of a rest that is their highest activity and a nothingness that is their being, and so forth (For Merton on these points see AT, 24; CGB, 267). But with Merton the paradox extends beyond his mystical elevations to include all the elements of his life and thought. "My life is almost totally paradoxical." "I find myself traveling toward my destiny in the belly of a paradox" (R, 16; SJ, 21).

But more than paradox is involved. Commentators have pointed to Merton's contradictions. (He would speak of his "self-contradictory hungers," and of "basic contradictions" within. One long-time monastic friend (J. E. Bamberger) would tell of "the Mertonian freedom from consistency"—he knew of no one less bothered about changing his mind. It should be noted that Merton had abundant occasion to be found changing his mind and being inconsistent, for he was a tireless writer. Before entering the monastery he considered writing a hundred books to say what he had to say. He often affirmed the mystical experience cannot be put into words, but his verbal output on mysticism was astounding—possibly greater than that of any other recognized mystic. Beyond the sixty books mentioned above, he published many uncollected articles, book reviews, prefaces, and about thirty-five hundred letters, while many conferences are now available on audio cassette. There remain many journals that cannot be published until twenty-five years after his death. These will clarify his personal experiences; they seem to be more personal than his published journals.[2] Yet all his writings are highly personal accounts showing a man of the modern world struggling to find his way through the ancient customs of monastic life.

The length of Merton's writing career would explain many inconsistencies—but not all.[3] Sometimes he would write inconsistent accounts of the same event: as in the famous passage of *Conjectures* telling of a visit to Louisville (see SMTM, 311–12; see also SMTM, 161). After his death many of his friends collaborated on a volume of testimonials, *Thomas Merton, Monk.* Three of the contributors tell of his inconsistency.[4] Such are the difficulties one faces in writing a systematic study of Thomas Merton—an author who warned against the "pretense of system."

[2]One of the few with access to these journals says they tell of Merton "seeking from God enlightenment on why he had never had a major mystical experience" (see James Laughlin in *Mert.ByThose,* 7).

[3]Some would occur in the same book: e.g., *New Seeds of Contemplation* has us born with our false identity and then creating it during our life.

[4]They were all fellow monks: J. E. Bamberger gives an example and adds, "Merton's writings team with such contradictory statements;" Dumont writes, his "sometimes contradictory enthusiasms were confusing;" T. Conner writes, "He would often make some point only later to assert what appeared to be diametrically opposed" (TM,M, 50, 126, 174).

In general, the change in Merton is from being a radically world-denying and triumphalist monk, a contemplative out of the world to his becoming a "world-affirming and broadly ecumenical person, a contemplative at the heart of the world" (Grayston, 12). To deal with this change I have tried to present the basic lines of Merton's development in the first two sections of chapter I. Yet beyond these evident changes there is also a striking unity in Merton's thought that should not be overlooked; concerns from his college days continued into his final years. This deeper unity became evident to me only as I worked with his texts. The four chapters deal with four issues that dominate his writing: Self, Contemplation, Freedom, and Other People. By considering these at length, I hope to offer a unified sense of the man I never met, but whom I seem to know as a friend. Here was an American telling of infused contemplation. I listened. And the wider world listened too: *The Seven Storey Mountain* was translated into sixteen languages and *Seeds of Contemplation* into fifteen. Seventeen years after his death a seven-hundred page biography of Merton rested for several weeks on the *New York Times* list of best sellers.

Most of Merton's books and many of his letters touch on mysticism in one form or another. Yet Merton did not use the term mystic (mysticism, mystical) with great frequency—he clearly preferred speaking of contemplation. He would generally restrict the term mysticism to contemplation in the strict sense, that is, infused contemplation, but occasionally he would use the term more widely. "Mysticism embraces the whole interior experience of a soul immersed in the Absolute" (AT, 62). The present study would have greater interest in the wider use—as there is little that can be said about the former. What follows is a somewhat systematic account of Merton's thought. Yet the author knows Merton opposed all systems and refused to be a systematic thinker.

Because the present study tries to identify the major lines of his thought, it does not consider the sources influential in his development. The achievement of Merton is that he could take ideas from ancient or unlikely texts, make them his own, and present them fully alive to the modern world. Shortly before entering the monastery, he had told of wanting to write "all about God in a new witty and pertinent way" that would reach the modern audience (MAG, 188). In this he was a striking success. Merton was always a voracious reader, immensely influenced by what he read. Before entering the monastery his religious interest was nourished by neo-scholastic philosophy and the religious poets, especially William Blake and Gerard Manley Hopkins. As a young monk Merton read widely in the Latin and Greek Fathers of the Church and in the medieval monastic tradition. Though he had some interest in Eastern mysticism before entering the monastery, it was only after 1950 that he began a serious study of non-Christian sources. Around 1957 his interest broadened to current events, an interest that continued until his death.

In the 1960s Merton began writing of the social issues that were dividing America, and civil-rights activists and anti-war protesters began heading to the Kentucky hills to consult a monk about strategies to get the United States out of Vietnam. But Merton challenged the activists with a contemplative question: "By what right do we protest?" They did not expect the question and some were annoyed, but soon they were looking beyond strategy to ask what it was all about. He made people think, when they did not believe it necessary. And in the midst of the confusion about an unpopular war, a troubled America came to appreciate the contemplation that should direct and change our action. Merton was doing what he did best: presenting the ultimate questions, and he made the modern world probe beyond the familiar. For deeper than the forces that were tearing the nation apart, he had found a unifying Power at "the center of America"—a Power holding the universe together. This his prose would try to show.

The present work tries to offer a unified account of the output of Merton. It quotes short phrases in abundance as often these convey the life of the man and testify to my own desire to present his message more strongly than my own. They also enable the reader to consult the passages that touch on the reader's interest. In drawing from the range of his works, I am aware of making little use of his poetry, for his poetry puzzles me and does not move me as does his prose. I was glad to find that his own favorite among his poems ("Elias-Variations on a Theme"; see RJ, 327) was one of the few I really liked. I use brief passages of it to introduce the chapters.

1

Self

Where the fields end
Thou shall be My friend
Where the bird is gone
Thou shalt be My son.

Thomas Merton became widely known in 1948 with the publication of his autobiography *The Seven Storey Mountain*. There he told of his dissipation at Cambridge, his studies at Columbia, his conversion to Catholicism, and his austere life as a Trappist monk. Merton was only thirty-three when his life-story was published, but he had not finished with autobiography: throughout twenty-seven years of monastic life he continued to publish detailed accounts of his doings. His abbot was concerned: "There is so much necessarily and unavoidably of the I, I, I" (RJ, 209). Most other mystics felt their personal histories were of no consequence. But Merton recorded his history in careful detail—while telling of losing his self. But if he really lost himself, could he continue to have a history? Without a self could he still speak or write with a highly distinctive voice?

The Writer and the Self

When Thomas Merton finished his master's degree at Columbia, he began teaching English at the Franciscan College of St. Bonaventure in upstate New York. Throughout the fall semester of 1941 he debated whether he should work at Friendship House, an outreach project in Harlem, or become a monk at Gethsemani, a Trappist monastery in Kentucky. In late November he came to his moment of decision:

> . . . if there is a choice for me between Harlem and the Trappists, I would not hesitate to take the Trappists. . . . That would be one place where I would have to give up *everything* . . . . Perhaps I cling to my independence, to the chance to write. . . . I must be prepared to give all these things up. It seems monstrous at the moment that I should consider my writing important enough even to enter into the question. . . . I return to the idea again and again: "Give up *everything,* Give up *everything!*" (SecJ, 222–223).

This account, probably written on the day of decision, shows Merton already aware of a conflict between monastic life and the writing that was so important. He made his decision and hurried from his room to tell it to a Franciscan priest who had only one question: "Are you sure you want to be a Trappist?" "Father, I want to give God everything" (SSM, 366). He returned to his room and wrote to the abbot of Gethsemani asking if he could come. On December 10, three days after the Japanese bombed Pearl Harbor, Thomas Merton left St. Bonaventure's to become a monk. He called his entrance "a civil and moral death;" he would lose himself; he was throwing away his "civil identity" (SJ, 240).

Merton had some familiarity with Trappist life, for he had visited the monastery the previous spring and his account of the visit gives a perspective on his decision to enter. He arrived at the monastery on Palm Sunday and soon went to the chapel where he saw the monks gathered "in the *anonymity* of their choir and the white cowls" (SSM, 325). He was impressed by the "liturgical anonymity" of their prayer. He was attracted by "the obscurity, the anonymity of this big Trappist family (R, 145). The meaning of anonymity was explained when he saw another "visitor" apply to enter as a postulant. The visitor would join the monks for communal prayer, and at first he stood out from the monks by his secular clothing. Then he too appeared in a cowl:

> . . . suddenly we saw him no more. He was in white. They had given him an oblate's habit, and you could not pick him

out from the rest. The waters had closed over his head, and he was submerged in the community. He was lost. The world would hear of him no more. He had drowned to our society and become a Cistercian (SSM, 325).

Running through these passages is the appeal of anonymity. But Harlem offered a similar appeal: there he could see himself part of the "huge, *anonymous mass* of the forgotten and the derelict" (SSM, 342). He was highly self-conscious as a writer; he dreaded the thought that he might become "high-priest" in a cult of himself as writer. He would renounce the life of the writer and become anonymous—in Gethsemani or Harlem.

The mystical tradition has many accounts of the mystic losing one's identity. But losing identity—seeking anonymity—is not confined to the mystics. Freud told of people being absorbed in "oceanic feelings," and Marx told of losing one's self in the masses of the oppressed. Merton wanted to lose himself for Christ, and the particular ocean or mass in which he would do so was a community of Trappists. While making his spring visit to the monastery, Merton wrote that the liturgy "is principally to kill us; in the drama (of the liturgy) we must die." (This passage was excised by his editor; in ms. dated April 9, 1941.) This "death" again suggests a passing away of the self and explains why he would consider his entrance to be "a civil and moral death." "It is a death, a true death, the death of a secular" (EEG, 27).

Merton would claim that a Trappist-Cistercian should seek to be the "least distinguished," to be "absolutely lost, ignored," to have "no . . . distinction that one can claim as one's own" (SJ, 196). As a novice he was excused from attending night prayers, but he tells of making a nuisance of himself asking to attend so he could be "the same as everybody else" (Cath. World: 1950, 428). Together the monks lived a "common life": each shared the same diet, the same time schedule, identical clothing, and a common dormitory. The accidents of their past were being "ironed out of them," and "everything they had was being sublimated and fused into the big vital unity" (R, 150). They renounced their individual tastes and all preoccupation with "their own ideas and judgments and opinions and de-

sires." This assisted the monks in coming to the selflessness required of the mystic. It appealed to Merton, but what would it
do to him as a writer? Should he lose concern for his "own
ideas and judgments and opinions," he might make a better
monk, but he would limit his ability to write original prose.

Merton compared entering the monastery to entering the
army. In each case one is given a uniform and loses the civilian
clothes that express one's individuality. "If it is a good monastery, he will be stripped of practically everything." For everything—even the self—is surrendered to God.

> Cistercian life strips the soul of everything that appeals
> (WAW, 82, 83). When a man becomes a Cistercian, he is
> stripped not only of his clothes, or part of his skin, but of his
> whole body and most of his spirit as well. And it is not all fin-
> ished the first day: far from it! The whole Cistercian life is an
> evisceration, a gutting and scouring of the human soul (R,
> 313).

Merton set about gutting and scouring his own soul with such
determination that he soon collapsed from physical and mental exhaustion.

Before he seriously considered entering the monastery, he
told of wanting to see himself in print. But this ambition
seemed to interfere with the supernatural life he was beginning
to know (SSM, 236). When he was making his decision to enter
the monastery, he thought of his writing and quickly judged it
monstrous that he should even consider the matter. But he did.
When he entered the monastery, he lost little time in telling his
superiors of his interest in writing. But as a novice he reflected,
"I used to love books and study, but God will want me to die to
all that. I used to want to be a writer, but God wants me to die
to all that." Writing would make his opinion, his perspective,
his self, stand apart from the other monks. Before entering the
monastery, he had had several small pieces published, and he
went apart with the text to glow over the result. "And the taste
of that pleasure is something that takes hold of you like a drug"
(*Renascence,* vol. 2, spring, 1950). This taste of ego-pleasure
left him distressed. He would explain that the creative author
can get caught into "a state of infatuated self-absorption"
(AmBenRev: 1960, 209).

Because of Merton's nervous exhaustion and collapse, he was unable to do physical work, so he was encouraged to translate some texts into English. This gave him no problem: "I translate pages of French without a question" (RJ, 16). In seeing his translation in print (*The Soul of the Apostolate*), he regarded it with mild indifference. He wondered what else there was for a Trappist to write and thought of the devotional pamphlets sold at the gatehouse of the monastery. The nature of monastic anonymity is evident in their titles: "the pamphlets bear the legend: 'A Trappist says . . .' 'A Trappist declares . . .' 'A Trappist implores . . .'" (SSM, 412).

Then Merton was asked to write the lives of several saintly Cistercians. They were to be published anonymously (WTW, x). But this turned out very different from writing a translation: "I was doing my own research and my own original writing." Now his prose was more or less original, yet his repetition of the pious formulas common in devotional writing gave these works a vague, impersonal quality. He would later regard this writing as "awful" and add "that is the way that I thought a monk was supposed to write." He was writing as "*a* monk"!

After writing of saintly Cistercians, he became involved in a project that could never be the work of an anonymous monk: an autobiography. Some older monks objected that monks did not write autobiographies, for they had renounced their earlier lives. But, eventually Merton's text was approved for publication with the understanding that the book would appear without the author's name. However, his literary agent, Naomi Burton (Stone), objected strongly and insisted that the anonymous monk be identified. He received permission from the abbot general of the Trappists to publish under his own name, and *The Seven Storey Mountain* became a run-away best seller.

Writing an autobiography is very different from translating the text of another, for the translator should suppress one's own opinion to express only what the author has written. Then, in writing of Cistercian saints, Merton used many devotional phrases not really his own. But his autobiography was highly distinctive and personal, and that was the problem. Was he not to lose himself? When Gandhi considered writing his autobiography, he was advised that autobiography was not part of the Hindu tradition; Hindu writings were largely anonymous. Several Christian saints have written autobiographies, notably St. Augustine. But though Augustine's autobiography had enormous influence on the centuries that followed, the Western Church had no other Christian autobiography until Abelard. In the Renaissance, St. Ignatius and St. Teresa wrote their life stories, but only with great reluctance. When pressured to do so they both maintained a certain distance: St. Ignatius spoke of himself as "the pilgrim," and St. Teresa referred to herself as "a certain woman." That is, they wrote of themselves in the third person. The difficulty that a "holy one" finds in writing an autobiography is that it gives significance to the historical self—while one tells of losing the self in God. St. Paul knew the difficulty and recounted his own mystic experience in the third person: "I know a man who . . . ." (2 Cor. 12:2).

Thomas Merton had immersed himself in the anonymity of Trappist life, only to find himself a national celebrity. His highly personal story made him stand out from the other monks with whom he wished to identify. He was known to the world, even though his identity would be unknown within the monastery. The present author talked with a monk who entered Gethsemani in the early 1950s; his decision to enter was influenced by reading Thomas Merton, yet he told of being a monk for almost two years before he knew which monk was Thomas Merton! This was monastic anonymity. When Merton took his religious vows, he told of "a deep and warm realization that I was immersed in my community" (SJ, 40). But as an original author he would have contrary feelings: "An author in a Trappist monastery is like a duck in a chicken coop." And longing to be like the others he said he "would give anything in the world to be a chicken instead of a duck" (SJ, 95). The author was in conflict with the anonymous monk.

The voice in Merton's autobiography was deeply Trappist and deeply his own. The combination was striking in a world wherein the sensitive author is alienated from all groups. Must not each author strive to have a distinctive voice? How could an author continue to be a monk without developing "his own ideas and judgments and opinions"? Merton began his monastic writing by repeating the "pious rhetoric" that was not particularly successful. But in the tension between the anony-

mous "monk" and the sensitive individual, Merton the author
was born. He would claim that "in order to become myself I
must cease to be what I always thought I wanted to be . . . in
order to live I must die." He had wanted to be a writer and this
was the death he believed he must die in entering the monastery, but by his every text he continued to live and affirm his
distinctive perspective. At the end of *The Seven Storey Mountain,* he told eloquently of his dilemma:

> . . . my vows should have divested me of the last shreds of
> any special identity. But then there was this shadow, this
> double, this writer who had followed me into the clois-
> ter. . . . He is supposed to be dead. But he stands and meets
> me in the doorway of all my prayers, and follows me into
> church. . . . He generates books in the silence that ought to
> be sweet with the infinitely productive darkness of contem-
> plation. And the worst of it is, he has my superiors on his
> side. They won't kick him out. I can't get rid of him. . . .
> Nobody seems to understand that one of us has got to die
> (SSM, 410).

The whole context of the passage is urging that the writer must
die. So in signing the rights of his autobiography over to the
Trappists Merton observed, "The royalties of the dead author
will go to the monastery."

But the dead author was very much alive and busily working
on his next book, *The Seeds of Contemplation.* Again the prose
is distinctive and fresh. But in the introduction Merton tried to
deny the evident originality of his own prose: he claimed the
work did "not contain a line that is new to the Catholic tradition;" it was only "the kind of thoughts that might have occurred to any Cistercian monk." And there is even the claim,
"This is the kind of book that writes itself almost automatically in a monastery." Many of his fellow Cistercians found
Merton's "kind of thoughts" very different from their own.
And no significant book is written "automatically." Merton
was unwilling to accept his own voice. He still wanted the anonymity of "A Trappist says . . . ."

This "death" of self is again suggested when *The Seeds*
speaks of the moment of contemplation: the soul is "annihilated," "it ceases to exist." Such phrases provoked considerable

criticism among Catholic philosophers, so in the next edition Merton explained that he was not speaking literally—he was only telling of his own experience.[5] *The Seeds* is hardly telling of the common monk, for it dealt with a problem that was distinctly his own: the problem of being both a contemplative and a writer: in order to write a contemplative "would have to withdraw from Him (God) and emerge from the depths before words and ideas would separate themselves out and take shape." "As soon as you attempt to make words of thoughts about it (contemplation) you are excluded—you go back into your exterior in order to talk" (SC, 140). Again there is the difficulty: Merton is trying to lose himself in God. But in order to write about losing himself he has to step back into the self he has lost to tell about it. In contemplation the self is said to be "absorbed and immersed" so that "selfhood no longer has any part"; one is "annihilated." But creating a text requires something very different. With every judgment one makes—and every judgment one publishes—one is affirming an individual perspective. "Pious rhetoric" can be more or less impersonal, but an original text cannot. In claiming that his book contained the thoughts of any monk, Merton was unwilling to acknowledge the striking originality of his own prose. He was still hoping for monastic anonymity.

Merton had admired the simplicity of the monks who had lost all preoccupation with "their own ideas and judgments and opinions." Those who surrender their opinions are more or less delivered from forming any opinions of their own. And this attitude aided contemplation, for the simplest way to contemplation is by following the "obedience and guidance of another." The contemplative will even develop "a hunger to be led and advised and directed by someone else;" "he comes to have a passion for obedience itself and for the renunciation of his own will and his own lights."

Soon Merton found himself caught in several strange dilemmas: First, he had taken on religious obedience: he had surrendered his judgment to another. But the one to whom he

---

[5] In a tape made in the middle sixties, Merton again spoke of "annihilation" and joked that the term would not be acceptable at The Catholic University. (*Contemplation and Renunciation,* Credence tapes).

surrendered has told him to write, that is, to judge! Further-
more, his contemplation gave him a passion to renounce his
own "lights." How can a writer function with such a passion?
He has wanted to die into the anonymity of the monastery, and
he has gained an international reputation. His problem centered on his identity as a writer: "What I write sticks to me
like flypaper."

Merton has claimed that creativity can involve one in "narcissism and self display"—the writer becomes high priest in
"the cult of himself" (Amer.Ben.Review, December, 1960,
201–202). This is the cult he wanted to avoid and the reason
that he saw writing opposed to his religious vocation: "I used
to be a writer, but God wants me to give up all writing." He had
decided to give up all writing and become a "rip-roaring Trappist" only to find his excess of zeal left him in a state of nervous
collapse. Writing translations gave him no problem, but problems appeared when asked to write original prose. "It is here
that I have really found many of the crosses that have so far
fallen me as a Cistercian" (*Renascence,* vol II, 2, 1950).

Merton's journal tells endlessly of the ongoing conflict of the
writer and the monk (SJon, 39, 43, 48, 61, 78, 95, 96, 124, 129,
153, 156): he would explain to himself that he did not have to
worry about the matter, for writing was "disinfected by obedience." But he was not satisfied and had to explain again: "It
ought to be quite clear that Reverend Father is set on my writing books." When the abbot general came from France to visit
the monastery, Merton brought up the matter with him and
was told "explicitly" and "under obedience" that he was to
continue writing. Still unable to find peace, he brought up the
matter with his abbot and was told to continue writing in spite
of his misgivings. The difficulty remained: "Since I have become a great success in the book business I have been becoming more and more of a failure in my own vocation" (SJon, 207).
In some sense he was both a writer and a monk and found both
identities in trouble: "If I were more immersed in the Rule of
St. Benedict . . . . If I were more absorbed in the presence of
God, I would be a better writer" (SJon, 233).

The return of his literary sensibility made it difficult for him
to listen to the common reading in the Chapter Room: "It is an
incantation of familiar sentences, stated in a way that is calcu-

lated to carry with it a certain enchantment to the Catholic," but it would mean nothing to someone outside the Church (SJon, 205-06). In short it was just more of the "pious rhetoric" that Merton himself had been writing. Some anonymous monk had assembled the pious thoughts that any monk might write—the things that might be written automatically in a monastery.

Merton's difficulties were aggravated when he began reading significant literary works. The *Notebooks* of Rilke caused him to reflect that

> monks do not seem to be able to write so well—and it is as if our professional spirituality sometimes veiled our contact with the naked realities inside us. It is a common failure of monks to lose themselves in a collective professional personality—to let themselves be cast in a mold (SJon, 245).

Merton had tried to assume this "collectivity professional personality" himself, only to find that his personal, literary sensitivities were drawing him apart from the mold, from any mold, from *anonymity*—and going apart from the mold is necessary if one is to contact the naked reality "inside." Merton was also finding it increasingly difficult to pray with the monks in choir—the place where he had first observed anonymity and its appeal.

Merton was ordained on May 26, 1949. Several weeks later while chanting the Gospel at community Mass, he became dizzy and fell to the floor. He was helped to his feet and tried to continue singing the Gospel, but he was still confused and had to be assisted from the altar. Several months later it was again his turn to chant the Gospel; he had difficulty breathing and his legs seemed to be turning into jelly. On finishing the Mass he asked not to serve again in public. He has left only cryptic phrases to explain the problem: "It was a sort of slow, submarine earthquake which produced strange commotions on the visible, psychological surface of my life." It was the effect of something that had already erupted "in the hidden volcano" (SJon, 226). A doctor ordered him to take an extended rest.

In terms of the text quoted above, Merton was coming into contact with the "naked realities inside," with that which was hidden by the "collective professional personality" he had tried to assume. He went through a "furnace of purification" that brought him in and out of the hospital and lasted until December 1950. Then he found a "spring of new life" in the midst of "abysmal testing and disintegration." He came to a very different sense of who he was.

The Merton that emerged would no longer want to "immerse" himself in his community nor be a chicken in a chicken coop. And he would no longer tell of a conflict between the writer and the monk. He announced a new commitment to "using my own words to talk about my own soul" (Pennington, TMBM, 90). And this he would do. He told of not wanting to divorce himself from the Catholic tradition, "but neither do I intend to accept points of that tradition blindly, and without understanding, and without making them really my own" (NMI, xiv). Now he was willing to accept his own perspective. The new Merton would look back on his years in the monastery and say: "My road has taken a new turning. It seems to me that I have been asleep for nine years—and that before that I was dead" (SJon, 315). His self was awake now and it would no longer be seeking "immersion" and "anonymity."

Before entering the monastery Merton had written an essay comparing the priestly life with the lay life. Those with a vocation to the priesthood were said to be the lucky ones, because "for them, from then on, everything is definite, is settled for them, they will have much guidance." Then he believed he would remain a layman, so he asked, "How can the general words of Christ be reduced to fit our particular cases?" (unpublished essay in files of Merton archives). In coming to the monastery he thought he would enter a life that was completely defined. His "definition" would be the same as all the others. But the common definition fell away and he found himself standing empty and alone. But he believed the change was for the better; he would ask, "Who is more poor in spirit than the man who takes the risk of standing on his own feet, who tries to realize his fallibility and struggles in his own conscience to realize the will of God?" But, Merton would add, if one fears this poverty of spirit he will join some existing power block that "fills his mind and his head with their jargon;" he covers his own "weakness by a wall of anonymity" (DQ, 106). Anonymity was no longer a goal—it was only a way of hiding the truth! Merton soon was saying there is "no need for a religious community of robots without minds, without hearts, without ideas and without faces" (CWA, 100).

Soon Merton would be challenging the other monks: "Are you going to stand on your own feet before God and the world and take full responsibility for your own life?" (CWA, 259). He would urge that as intelligent human beings we ought "to stand on our own feet" (RU, 59). A free human being should have the "power to stand on his own feet" (NM, 105). On the day of his death in Bangkok, he gave a talk that included a parable that ended with the same advice, "You can no longer rely on being supported by structures." "From now on everybody stands on his own feet." This is the Merton that emerged from the disintegration. The new Merton would have difficulty with the familiar structures and any attempts at defining a monk. He would speak his own mind and say what he sees. He will refuse to be an impersonal author, the "voice of Trappist silence," or the voice of anyone but himself. He knew that standing alone would bring anxiety, but this was the anxiety that led to compassion. He was seeing the monastic vocation in a very different way:

> When one is immersed in a wide and free-flowing stream of articulate tradition, he can easily say more than he knows and more than he means and get away with it. One can be content to tell his brethren in Christ what they devoutly desire and expect, no more and no less (DQ, 34).

Merton would soon be telling his brethren more than they desired or expected. This too would have its problems. But the writer who emerged from the disintegration would speak only for himself.

The Paradox of Delivery

Shortly after his ordination Merton was put to teaching the young monks. He warned them against clinging to official standards of good conduct only to evade their real identity. He told them not to assume a generally accepted personality, but create their own selves by their judgments and free choices (CWA, 77–78). He would rework an earlier text that told of *finding* one's identity to read that we must "share with God the work of *creating* the truth of our identity" (NSC, 32). He made it clear that he was no longer trying to lose his identity: for "in the contemplative life above all, lack of identity is a disaster" (CWA, 93).

Now Merton would claim the belief that the monk should dissolve his personality "in a formless mass without any individual character at all" is a perversion of monasticism (SL, 42). Yet this dissolution was what he himself had tried. Now he was warning against any "submersion of the personality in the social whole" (MJ, 79). The "immersion in the mass of other men" was only a temptation that would leave one in "a formless sea of irresponsibility" (NSC, 54). Merton judged it a flagrant violation of the human person "to renounce one's autonomy to the point of abandoning all spontaneous reflection, intellection, volition, even feeling" (CWA, 87). To attempt this renunciation is "gravely damaging" and ultimately unworkable. The whole seeking of "anonymity" and a "highly respectable nothingness" was dismissed as an evasion of maturity (CWA, 72); and the monastic choir—whose anonymity appealed so strongly to the young Merton—was called "the scene of much depersonalization." Merton warned the monks lest they become "mere automata praising God like machines" (CWA, 70, 95; MJ, 70–71).

When the abbot visitor came from France, Merton was told he was too independent, *un esprit particulier* unwilling to enter *dans la moule.* His abbot would preach to the community on the value of "conformity" and of "running with the herd," and Merton believed that the phrases were to himself. But he continued to state what he saw. He even looked back on the days of monk-and-writer-in-conflict and announced that his writing was a "necessary outlet" for the closeness of community life (letter to Leclercq, Oct. 5, 1959). He told his abbot, "If ever I were forbidden to write, I would soon land in a mental hospital" (Fox writing in TMM, 155). In short, the duck in the chicken coop was making ducklike noises for all the chickens to hear.

Merton would no longer try to be the "good monk" or even the "good Catholic." He would publicly criticize the decisions of his abbot and criticize the Catholic hierarchy for their support of the Vietnam war. He blamed Catholic moral theologians for arguing over trifles and ignoring the "polite, massively organized, white-collar murder machine that threatens the world with destruction" (FV, 7). He claimed that for twenty centuries Christianity had "been taking Caesar for God and God for Caesar" (DQ, 61). As a young monk he had praised everything monastic and everything Catholic (including the Inquisition!). His later writing seemed to focus on the faults of monasticism and Catholicism. Much of his writing on war and peace was not approved for publication, but it circulated privately and he became well known among various peace groups of the sixties. But again he would stand on his own feet: "If a pacifist is one who believes that all war is always morally wrong and always has been wrong, then I am not a pacifist" (NA, 67). When someone from the Catholic Peace Fellowship set fire to himself in front of the United Nations in New York, Merton asked that his name be taken off the list of Fellowship sponsors. (After considerable clarification he allowed his name to remain.)

During the latter years of his life Merton wrote many essays defending the individual against the pressures of the group. In these essays Merton seemed to be defending the autonomy that once he had tried to lose. He introduced one collection of essays as a defense of "the rights of man against the encroachments and the brutality of massive power structures" (FV, 4). Another collection would deal with "the relation of the person to the social organization" (DQ, viii). Both collections dealt with a wide variety of topics, but through them all Merton was telling of the oppressive "power structures" and the "social organization" in which he had tried to lose himself. He told of wanting "to be free from a sort of denominational tag." He wanted to move out of the monastery building and live as a hermit, and he would speak of himself as a "non-monk," as a "solitary explorer," or a "tramp." A friend would call him a "lone warrior." He was going out of his way *not* to be immersed in his monastic community.

Merton's prose also changed: he would avoid the "incantation of familiar phrases" that monasticism, Catholicism, or any other group can develop. He warned against the religious prose that plays "checkers with a certain number of familiar devotional cliches" (BW, 55). He would make fun of his earlier language: mystique, "suggests an emotional icing on an ideo-

logical cake"; the hidden life, "a life of tranquility which a chosen minority can enjoy at the price of a funny costume and a
few prayers" (NA, 250–51). He wanted no more of the "select
groups" and "closed circles" that fill people's minds with "mental cliches, non-descriptive linguistic rubbish, sentimental jargon." He was through with "pious rhetoric" and determined to
speak in another way: "free from the dictates of partisan
thought patterns" and unwilling to write "a set piece dictated
by (his) social situation" (DQ, 17). He had resolved to stand
apart from "immersion in the general meaninglessness of
countless slogans and cliches repeated over and over again."
He was determined to be himself and stand on his own feet for
real (HGL, 511). He would warn his fellow monks: "When you
say 'I think' it is often not you who think, but 'they'—it is the
anonymous authority of the collectivity speaking through your
mask" (Cist.Stud. vol xviii, 1983, 3). He would avoid any
"anonymous authority" and speak without a mask.

In 1947 Merton had written an essay on the conflict between
the contemplative and the poet. The poet was said to come to
the point wherein he must renounce poetry to enter more
deeply into contemplation. At this point the poet was to make
a "ruthless and complete sacrifice of his art" (FA, 110). Such
was "the simplest, the safest and the most obvious way" of re-
solving the conflict of vocations. Merton allowed this would ap-
pall those who do not appreciate the difference between nature
and grace. But soon after publication of this essay he was having
second thoughts: he wrote to a friend of seeing things "in a
strangely different light" (RJ, 22). Basically, each poet should
follow the individual destiny given one by God. In October
1958 Merton published a "reappraisal" of this early text. And
the reappraisal would *not* call on the poet to make the radical
sacrifice.

In the revised essay of 1958, Merton would repeat the
phrases that told of poetic intuitions interfering with contemplation. But now the interference would only *tempt* the poet to
believe he "must consent to the ruthless and complete sacrifice
of his art" (R, 412). Now the sacrifice would *seem* to be essential. Merton even allowed that *logic* might dictate this conclusion (should not one reject the natural for the supernatural and

the temporal for the eternal?). But then *"human* logic" should not have the final word!

> . . . when one has experience in the strange vicissitudes of the inner life, and when one has seen something of the ways of God, one remembers that there is a vast difference between the logic of men and the logic of God. There is indeed no human logic in the ways of interior prayer, only Divine paradox. . . . experience teaches us that the most perfect choice is not always that which is most perfect in itself. The most perfect choice is *the choice of what God has willed for us,* even though it may be, in itself, less perfect, and indeed less "spiritual" (R, 413; italics in text).

This "reappraisal" offers a surprising solution: God has his own logic according to which one might be required to do what is *"less perfect"* and *"less spiritual"*! Merton continued to believe that mystical prayer enables one to receive divine light, and he would still believe that the sacrifice of writing seems a small price to pay for this light. But now Merton was claiming that all Christian writers are not confronted with what seems an inescapable conclusion. One individual might indeed be called to sacrifice one's art in order to enter deeply into contemplation. While another is called to be an artist. In that case "he should sacrifice his aspirations for a deep mystical life and be content with the lesser gifts with which he has been endowed by God." It is all a matter of the individual. Some poets are called to sacrifice a deep mystical life to be poets; this is what God asks of them. Merton seemed to be telling of his own situation: he would sacrifice something of the mystical life in order to write. And the justification he gave is that one cannot simply follow an *a priori* principle about what is best, rather the mystic is dealing with God and God does what He pleases with whom He pleases. And Merton believed he was called to write, even to the detriment of his contemplation. In the meantime he allowed that the conflict between the artist and the mystic remained:

> . . . at a certain point in the interior life, the instinct to create and communicate enters into conflict with the call to mystical union with God. But God himself can resolve the

conflict. And he does. Nor does he need any advice from us in order to do so (R, 414).

God simply wills different things for different individuals. And God can lead one in a way that is "less perfect." This is termed a "paradox." Merton continued to see the opposition between the mystic and the writer, but he accepted that he was called to be a writer. God does not follow the logic of men. He does not deal with anonymous monks or anonymous poets; God deals only with individuals.

Since Merton would affirm his independence and no longer wanted to be the anonymous monk, one might ask about the danger of narcissism, of ego-pleasure, the danger of "infatuated self-absorption," of being "high-priest" in a cult of one's self, of "self-idolatry"—all of which Merton had warned can afflict the writer. Merton had discovered another way of losing himself apart from immersion in a group. He called it Zen. He found it great for "cracking idols."

In December 1949 as Merton was sinking into the extended disintegration that followed his ordination, he was walking near his monastery when he came to a new and vivid awareness:

> These clouds low on the horizon, the outcrops of hard yellow rock on the road, the open gate, the perspective of fenceposts leading up the rise to the sky, and the big cedars tumbled and tousled by the wind. Standing on rock. Present. The reality of the present and of solitude divorced from past and future. . . . My love for everybody is equal, neutral and clean. No exclusiveness. Simple and free as the sky, because I love everybody and am possessed by nobody, not held, not bound. In order to be not remembered or even wanted I have to be a person that nobody knows. They can have Thomas Merton. He's dead. Father Louis—he's half dead too. For my part my name is that sky, those fence posts, and those cedar trees (SJ, 246–47).

Merton wrote this passage shortly after a worker at the monastery had given the monks a talk on Zen. The passage illustrates well what Merton meant by the term. Zen was not a foreign religion (Buddhism was merely the culture in which Zen happened to develop). In itself Zen is a simple and direct awareness of the immediate present. It is an awareness apart from all interpretation and meaning; it is free of all teachings; it does not take "refuge behind a screen of conceptual prejudices and verbalistic distortions" (TMDP, 121).

Merton read the works of Daisetz Suzuki and found himself in "profound and intimate agreement" (HGL, 561). Merton's understanding of Zen could be summed up in three brief denials: (1) Zen makes no judgment., (2) Zen has no purpose., and (3) Zen allows neither ego nor denominational label.

1. *Zen makes no judgment.* Zen masters have insisted that in Zen there is "neither affirming or denying" (MZM, 131). As long as one is given to distinguishing, judging, categorizing, classifying, and even contemplating, one is imposing something on what is immediately present—one is filtering what is present through some system of names and ideas (Z, 53). Zen is the quest for direct and pure experience freed from all thought systems and verbal formulas. Zen simply regards; it "does not add any comment, any interpretation, any judgment, any conclusion." All of these distort what is simply there.

2. *Zen has no purpose.* Merton believed that Americans were obsessed with purpose. He saw them unable to appreciate the present in their concern for where it will lead and what it will mean; it followed that they could never be satisfied with what they have. Merton recommended the "purposeless life," what Zen refers to as "filling the well with snow." Merton hoped his drawings would show him to be "inconsequent," and he rejoiced in "the meaninglessness of the rain" (RU, 181). "No one seems to know how useful it is to be useless" (WCT, 59).

3. *Zen allows neither ego nor group identity.* Zen is a "seeing" without a seer. When a perception is pure, there is no ego; the ego appears only when one tries to integrate the present into the past or the future. But when one sees apart from memory or purpose, there is no ego. Zen is a pure awareness apart from subject and object. "Descartes made a fetish out of the mirror in which self finds itself. Zen shatters it" (CGB, 285). A Zen enlightenment occurs, but no one is enlightened. Zen is free of denominational labels. A Zen man is free of structures

and "external supports and enthusiasms" and does not wear the mask of any organization (Z, 45–46). *no labels or masks*

The best way of understanding this brief account of Zen is to consider the extended passage of Merton quoted above (Merton seeing rock, fenceposts and cedars). The passage includes (1) no judgment: he names clouds, yellow rocks and cedars, but only in phrases, not in sentences. (2) Things are there, but he makes nothing of them. To do this would give them a meaning and a future purpose whereby they would lose the simplicity of being what they are. There is "Present" divorced from past and future. (3) His secular ego (Thomas Merton) has died, and his religious identity (Father Louis) is about to do the same. He has transcended the difference between subject and object: "my name is that sky, those fenceposts." He does not identify with any group: "My love for everybody is equal, neutral and clean."

Earlier Merton had sought to lose himself by being immersed into the anonymity of a group; now he is immersing himself in the anonymity of trees, sky, and fenceposts. Earlier he had wanted to die to the knowledge of all created things. But with his recovery and change in attitude, he would start observing the small details of nature. He would take photos of dried leaves and weatherbeaten rocks and claim his camera was a Zen camera—it recorded what was there and made no judgment. For it is in making judgments that one gives rise to the ego self.

On the night before his fatal accident in Bangkok, Merton told a friend, "Zen and Christianity are the future." Merton would often speak of these two together. For they are the two ways that he tried to lose himself. First, he tried to lose himself into the anonymity of the Trappists (whom he regarded as the Christian ideal). Then, he tried to lose himself in immediate experience (Zen). If his early writing spoke with unrestrained enthusiasm for the wonders of Trappist life (see WS, 21), his later writing spoke with unrestrained enthusiasm for nature (Czeslaw Milosz has pointed out that Merton never spoke of evil or cruelty in nature). Now nature—not the Trappists— was idealized. *nature*

Thus, Merton had two ways of losing himself (first, into the group and, then, into immediate experience), but the sequence of these ways is also important. The loss in a group comes first. This is the sequence found in a Zen monastery: one begins by becoming part of an authoritarian group (these monasteries were originally associated with the training of the Samurai); one first merged one's self into a group identity. "Chinese and Japanese Zen both in fact flourished in extremely disciplined and authoritarian cultures." Though they spoke of the discovery of "autonomy," this discovery occurred only after "an intensely strict and authoritarian training" (Z, 46). (Merton's Zen enlightenment occurred only after a similar training.) Merton had no use for popular forms of Zen that did not recognize the importance of an authoritarian training (authority unites a group). Daisetz Suzuki agreed. Thus, one must begin by a surrender to authority/group (and in the process ignore immediate experience); it is only then that one proceeds to Zen: a discovery of immediate experience.

Merton's involvement with both Christianity and Zen show an unwillingness to judge (the [1] point considered above). He would explain: to judge is to take a Godlike view: "the act of judging is an act by which we set ourselves as unique, 'outside' the common run of beings, as something totally special and apart" (CWA, 67). By making judgments we are establishing a "spurious identity" apart from what we judge. Merton can be seen to avoid this "identity" in two ways: First, he would identify so deeply with the tradition of Christian monasticism that he would give it voice; he would not speak for himself. His "voice," his "spurious identity," had died in entering the monastery. When he began writing again, it was the anonymous prose that he believed "a monk," "a Trappist," should write. Consider the following:

> What mute, half-helpless acts of loving adoration and submission in the darkness of faith! Probably He (God) struck some hearts with deep shafts of consolation, and spoke some words of kindness that brought tears to the eyes (EEG, 81).

This is the pious rhetoric that Merton would later describe as awful; it is the professional piety that ignored the naked spiritual reality inside.

But Merton's Zen awakening would also affect his prose: under its influence he would sometimes string together momentary impressions that say nothing.

> Cries louder and louder, until he screams high "hellos" that fly beyond Kanchenjunga. Gasps. Despairing cockcrows. Yelps. Hound yells. Pursues a distant fading voice. Over far wires speeds the crazed hound (AJ, 160).

This "Zen prose" resembles the Japanese haiku. It is immediate experience recorded without comment. The practitioner of Zen also has difficulties in being an effective writer: How can one write prose while "neither affirming or denying"? How can one have no purpose while industriously producing books? Both judging and producing strengthen one in one's ego identity, and this is what Merton wanted to lose in entering the monastery. The one with no judgments of one's own is often regarded as a no one, for the self (in the worldly sense) comes into being by making personal judgments. First, to avoid judging Merton started taking the judgments of monastic tradition as his own; then, with an interest in Zen he again avoided judging; he simply recorded the data.

The two examples of Merton's prose quoted above are very different, but both were written by someone unwilling to judge, to have an opinion of one's own. In the first example Merton had surrendered his judging self to the group; *its* judgments—not his own—are what he has written. In the second example Merton has surrendered his judging self to immediate experience; the unjudged data is simply recorded. Both types of prose are ineffective, and the reason is the same: good prose should give one a sense of the writer or speaker. The teachers of Zen would warn: it is the act of "affirming or denying" that gives rise to the self. Merton wrote much good prose, but only when he had not entirely lost himself; only when he stood on his "own feet before God and the world and (assumed) responsibility"—for his own text—did he write well.

Merton had warned of the danger of forming a cult of one's self, a very real danger for any original author—especially if the author is successful. To avoid the "infatuated self-absorption" that had seized him like a drug, Merton adopted two forms of "self-emptying," but neither was entirely successful (see CWA, 87 and Z, 76). That Merton was partially able to succeed in each gave character to his prose; first, his early prose was able to state the monastic ideal with a power that came from his monastic involvement; and his later prose described the natural world with a similar power. By virtue of these partial "immersions," he was able to speak with a voice that was wider than his ego.

To tell of his situation as monk and writer, Merton would speak of paradox—the paradox that is central to the Christian life. Christ told his followers to lose their self (life) for him, and thereby they would find their self (life). In the early days of Christianity, the phrase was applied to the martyr. Soon the monk was also seen as a martyr; he too would surrender everything—monastic life was even called "evangelical death." This was the "death" that appealed to the young Merton as he entered the monastery with great enthusiasm. Perhaps his enthusiasm would have remained if he had not been encouraged to write. Writing hastened his crisis, for by all that he wrote Merton was giving himself a distinct identity. By each of his judgments he was separating himself from the common opinion of the group in which he had attempted submersion.

As a writer struggling to express what he saw and at the same time express the mind of the group, he brought himself into the depths of "disintegration." (During this time he was working on *The Ascent to Truth*. The following chapter will argue that in *The Ascent* Merton tried to lose himself into the scholastic philosophy then so important among Catholics. He would later regard *The Ascent* as his "emptiest book.") In finally being at peace with his writing, he would discover that losing oneself "paradoxically is not self-alienation" but "self realization" (CWA, 72). This is the very paradox that is at the heart of Christianity and is integral to Christian mysticism. Merton's "Reappraisal" best explains where he found himself: "There is indeed no human logic in the ways of interior prayer, only Divine paradox" (R, 413). By this paradox he accepted the writer-self that had died.[6] Merton's account of losing his

---

[6] I have dealt with this same paradox elsewhere: Sartre (writing about Flaubert) has claimed, "a great writer is always something of a Lazarus: he undergoes the common lot, he dies and begins to smell; at that time Someone intervenes who snaps his

writer-self and then finding it could be seen as a contemporary form of the losing and finding of self presented in the Gospel. And the prose of Thomas Merton, some of which comes from the self-lost (both examples quoted above) and some from the self-lost-and-found (most of his writing), can enable one to sense the meaning of the cryptic Gospel phrase that tells of losing and finding one's self.

It would seem Merton wrote his best prose when living the paradox. If people can relate to this prose, it is because everyone knows the tension of having a group allegiance and yet wanting to speak with one's own voice. And everyone knows the tension of being true to the data and at the same time shaping it to make of it a modicum of sense. These were the tensions that gave rise to the effective prose of Thomas Merton. Merton's struggles to lose himself in a group or in the experience of the moment make memorable prose. And they help clarify the Gospel paradox.

Appearing as a Catholic monk and telling of the wonders of Zen had its difficulties, but Merton spoke of it as "the contra-

fingers, time is reversed like an hourglass, he rises full of genius." See *Sartre & the Sacred,* 149. The writer-as-Lazarus parallels Merton's favorite scriptural image for himself, the writer-as-Jonah: both Lazarus and Jonah were symbols of a death and resurrection. David Cooper claims to show a "darker side of Merton" by urging that Merton had a carefully worked-out strategy wherein he would erect barriers that he would then overcome and emerge as writer (TMAD, 33). Though impressed by Cooper's case, I believe Cooper ignores Merton's relationship to God in an eagerness to show Merton a humanist all along the way.

Merton's death and resurrection as a writer can be understood more simply as a reflection of the poet he so much admired, Gerard Manley Hopkins. Merton's conversion was motivated by reading Leahy's account of the conversion of Hopkins. While reading this account one rainy evening Merton was moved to go out searching for a priest (SSM, 215). Shortly after Hopkins became Catholic he began considering religious life—as did Merton. Hopkins (again as recorded in Leahy) "resolved to write no more, as not belonging to my profession, unless it were by the wish of my superiors." He believed religious life would allow him to write "nothing or little in the verse way," but he could write religious prose. On November 6, 1865, Hopkins wrote in his diary, "on this day I resolved to give up all beauty until I had His leave for it." Is this not the model for Merton? Hopkins burned many of his poems before entering the Jesuits, so Merton burned much of his writing before entering the Trappists (see Cooper, TMAD, 63). As Merton was motivated to convert by reading of Hopkins' conversion, the motivation would continue. Like Hopkins, Merton needed superiors to tell him to write. And, again like Hopkins, Merton had more religious problems in writing poetry than he did in writing prose. It is hard to believe that Hopkins was not an ongoing model for Merton.

diction I have to live with" (AJ, 305). Contradictions (or paradoxes) remained and he acknowledged them with humor: "How useful it is to be useless." He was not entirely free from a fair measure of egoism. He would complain that his literary identity adhered to him like flypaper, but on a trip away from the monastery he announced to tourists on a California beach that he was Thomas Merton. In his final days he industriously edited his letters and cooperated in setting up the Thomas Merton Study Center at Bellarmine College. He saw the humor in it all: "What a comedy. But I like it and cooperate wholeheartedly because I imagine it is for real. That I will last. That I will be a person studied and commented upon" (Griffin, FE, 160).

The following section will deal in a more philosophical way with the problem of the self in the writings of Merton. But these somewhat philosophic writings should not be considered apart from the human individual who continued to have a lively self with its friendships and resentments, its nobility and foibles. If Merton never fully resolved the problem of the self on a theoretical level (see Carr, SWS, 3, 62, 131), the same could be said for the self with which he lived.

A Philosophy of the Individual and the Person

While still a nonbelieving student at Columbia, Merton read Aldous Huxley's *Ends and Means,* a study of mysticism that told of conflict between the flesh and the spirit. The work revolutionized Merton's thinking (SSM, 185). Then, following his conversion in 1938, he read several books by a contemporary Neo-scholastic philosopher, Jacques Maritain, which again told of a conflict between flesh and spirit. (For the influence of Maritain on Merton see SSM, 203–4, 277; TMA, 134; SMTM, 117; AT, x; CGB, 6, 182, 188, 270, 314, 348; FV, 191; SD, 115; SCh, 6, 14, 31, 47, 114, 129, 160, 183, 190, 191, 306, 312, 318, 322, 325).

Maritain would speak of everyone having "two poles:" a material pole and a spiritual pole. Maritain called the material pole the *individual* and associated it with the ego, egoism and bodily needs; he called the spiritual pole the *person* and associated it with creativity, freedom, goodness and love. Maritain believed all people lived in a tension between the two.

> If the development of the human being follows the direction of *material individuality,* he will be carried in the direction of the "hateful ego," whose law is to *snatch,* to absorb for one-self. In this case, personality as such will tend to adulterate, to dissolve. If, on the contrary, the development follows the direction of *spiritual personality,* then it will be in the direction of the generous self of saints and heroes that man will be carried. Man will really be a person, in so far as the life of spirit and of freedom will dominate in him that of passion and of the senses (*Scholast. & Pol.,* 66).

Following Maritain, Merton would frequently contrast "the individual" with "the person": the individual is part of the material universe and its determinisms, while the person is the image of God, creative and free. Merton would link this duality with St. Paul's duality of the "old man" and the "new man" and with St. Bernard's duality of the "false self" and the "true self." Merton developed many new names for these two "selfs": on a single page he contrasted the "worldly self" with the "true inner self," the "destructive ego" with the "mysterious inner self," and the "contingent ego" with "one's inviolate and eternal reality" (NSC, 38). But most of the time Merton used the terminology of Maritain: the individual and the person.

> We must remember that this superficial "I" is not our real self. It is our 'individuality' and our 'empirical self' but it is not truly the hidden and mysterious person in whom we subsist before the eyes of God. The "I" that works in the world, thinks about itself, observes its own reactions and talks about itself is not the true "I" that has been united to God in Christ (NSC, 7).

This second "I" (the person) is hidden, unnamed and unrecognized in society as we know it today.

Merton would often associate the "individual" with the "I" that Descartes found in reflective consciousness and led Descartes to his claim, *Cogito ergo sum* (CGB, 181, 265, 285; NSC, 8–9; Z, 22–28, 68; TMA, 131, 132; HGL, 494; SCh, 167; see SD, 52; VC, 194 and Carr, SWS, 31, 90). Merton believed that Descartes' claim situated our identity in the act of reflection and this left us alienated from our own inner depths; one was left to seek one's identity within one's thoughts. The Cartesian was trying to know the self objectively. And in endless contexts Merton insisted that the true self cannot reflect on itself; it is apart from all subject-object dichotomies. More than any other quality, this *in*ability to reflect on itself is the mark of the person. Thus, Merton considered the subject-object dualism developed by Descartes the root of human alienation.

For Merton the *cogito* is not the starting point for philosophy—the starting point is contemplation. To contemplate at all we must renounce the *cogito* and no longer "clench our minds upon themselves, as if thinking made us exist" (MJ, 223). Then in contemplation we would come to a simple and direct awareness: *SUM,* I Am. Then one is aware of dwelling in God as a relation to God and to all that is. Contemplation does not leave us cramped upon ourself, for it does not start with the thinking, self-aware subject, but from Being itself prior to the subject-object division. This is possible for "underlying the subjective experience of the individual self there is an immediate experience of Being" (Z, 23). This is totally non-objective (and non-subjective) and totally different from the *cogito* of Descartes wherein one becomes aware of one's self as an object of sorts. It is an immediate experience and is radically different from what Descartes set up as immediate experience. It is not "consciousness *of*" but *pure consciousness* in which the subject as such is said to disappear (Z, 24). Here one is aware of one's self as "a self-to-be-dissolved in self-giving, in love, in 'letting-go,' in ecstasy, in God." One has come to the place that God has commanded to be left empty: "the center, the existential altar which simply 'is'" (NSC, 13). Here there is "no division between subject and object. . . . He IS and this reality absorbs everything else" (NSC, 267). One cannot speak of this awareness with objective clarity, for it is the "immediate experience of a ground which transcends experience" (Z, 24).

The starting point makes all the difference. And "the basic reality is being itself, which is one in all concrete existents, which shares itself among them and manifests itself through them." Thus we should start with the "splendor of being and unity—a splendor in which (one) is one with all that is" (FV,

221). Descartes located certainty in his *cogito,* but Merton appealed to this ground of being for "a natural certainty that says that insofar as we exist we are penetrated through and through with the sense and reality of God" (MJ, 222). This can be expressed in either religious or philosophic terms.

If one begins with one's own reflexive consciousness instead of with the metaphysical intuition of Being, Merton claimed, Being is reduced to an abstract concept that the subject considers. And this is precisely what Being is not. But since Descartes had set up the ego found in the *cogito* as the measure of truth, he ruled out the possibility of a direct intuition of Being—and Being became an abstract notion. Again appealing to Maritain, Merton claimed that Being includes a "basic unity of subject and object" (Z, 68). In Being, both are one. If we do not start philosophy with Being, reality becomes subordinate to the concept we have of ourselves; then locked within our private world we have no reason to respond to anything else. We have become the self-subsistent starting point and end point, and our abstractions set the conditions for what is real. The whole Cartesian system has arranged it so that the "thinking, observing, measuring and estimating 'self' is absolutely primary" (Z, 22). One has subordinated the whole of reality to the "superficial ego" and thereby blocked out the experience of "the deeper meaning of our own identity" (CGB, 265). One has locked oneself in a subjective prison from which one tries to manipulate the world and one's body. The body is seen as a machine which "we regulate, tune up and feed with all kinds of stimulants and sedatives" (FV, 112). Our ego-image has become the absolute; this is "the idolization of reflexive consciousness" (CGB, 285). While the lonely ego is left to pick and pry "in the isolation of its own dull self analysis" (NMI, 34).

Descartes had argued to an objective image of God, and many Christians accepted Descartes and held to the image by an act of the will. But one cannot hold to an abstraction indefinitely. Merton saw the present generation realizing this, many centuries after Descartes. So now we speak of the death of God, but we are referring only to the abstract God Descartes bequeathed to us, a God that was dead from the beginning. By starting philosophy with reflection, we have set ourselves into a world without God, and the present generation acknowledges

the fact. In such a world one is left to affirm one's individuality
in opposition to the individuality of everyone else. This individual with its bodily form, emotions, appetites, and needs has
been made the "basic and indubitable reality to which everything else must be referred." Then the world is seen as a "multi-
plicity of conflicting and limited beings, all enclosed in the
prison of their own individuality" (FV, 200). In this immense
conflict each ego competes by asserting itself at the expense
of the others. A situation implicit in starting philosophy with
the *cogito.*

Merton believed that the true Christian idea of the human
starts with a "mystical consciousness" of God and the human
together. God has created us in his own image and this non-
reflective consciousness should be the basis of our understanding of the human. The Church has always taught that one
cannot know the human without some knowledge of God
(TMA, 131). But today Merton saw people developing systems
of thought that start from the purely human. They develop a
psychological or sociological system wherein God is irrelevant.
Some continue to speak of God, but what they have created is
"a sort of secular cake with a Christian icing" (TMA, 131).
Their difficulty goes back to the Cartesian starting point that
made the reflexive individual the basis of everything else.
Then one believes, "I define myself by negating others."
Merton saw this individualism to be radically opposed to the
Bible and the Christian tradition. And he believed American values were formed with this understanding, so that now
we think of ourselves as "billiard balls bumping into each
other" with no real interrelationships. This gave rise to the eco-
nomics of Adam Smith whereby Americans tried to become
rich and independent while obeying the traffic laws.

The Christianity of the eighteenth and nineteenth centuries
was seen to develop a "baptized" version of Descartes and
Adam Smith (TMA, 132). Christians were urged to lift the individualist understanding to the "supernatural plane" and
"have" charity for other individuals. But the starting point remained the individual and that was a basic mistake: charity became extrinsic to one's reality. "The Christian conscience goes
much deeper than that, because it is the self in Christ, the self
belonging to Christ" (TMA, 134). This must be the starting

point, a self-knowledge that involves more than the self, for such is the truth of who we are.

We cannot begin with an individualist understanding of our self and then add that we are Christians, for that would mean that Christ came as an individual to baptize *individuals*—and union in Christ would have no meaning. The reflective individual can never be "the 'I' who can stand in the presence of God and be aware of him as a 'Thou.' For this 'I' there is no clear 'Thou' at all" (Cist.Stud. vol xviii [1983] 4). For this "I" other people are merely extensions or reflections of one's own self. We have started with the individual. But "we don't really find out who we are until we find ourselves in Christ and in relation to other people." We are not individuals, we are persons, and "a person is defined by a relationship with others." Our personal identity comes to light "only when it fully confronts the 'other'" (NM, 46). Our existence is in relationship. This truth is discovered in contemplation. But the ego found in the *cogito* is unable to contemplate.

During his final years Merton would speak of finding ourselves in the "hidden ground of Love" wherein we are all united (HGL, 115; HR, 112; OB, 33). By this hidden ground Merton meant that "you push the thing as far as it will go and there is love" ("Life & Contemplation," tape). This would be the "ground" wherein we discover our selves forming a human community in God. Merton would tell his readers, "I seek to speak to you, in some way, as your own self." For Merton believed he and his reader shared a common inner depth wherein each could hear the "One who lives and speaks in both of us" (HR, 67). If we are conscious of our own depths, we will discover that we are all united in Love. In dialogue we will find "that we are both Christ" (HGL, 115, 387). Merton agreed with those who speak of "God as the ultimate self, who is the Self of every self" (VC, 67). But this would make no sense to the Cartesian.

Merton told of coming into the world with a false self, of being born with a mask that was selfish and self-centered. But that is to say he was born in sin. He continued,

> as long as I am no longer anybody else than the thing that was born of my mother, I am so far short of being the person

> I ought to be that I might as well not exist at all. In fact it were better for me that I had not been born (NSC, 34).

Yet this illusion is the self I want to be; it is a self that wants to exist apart from God's love. Here Merton speaks of being *born* with this illusion; later in the same book he calls it a "self-constructed illusion" (NSC, 280). But, born or constructed, we add to what might be our original falsity. We clothe the empty nothing of an image with power and honor in order to make ourselves visible. But we also find our individuality must compete with the individuality of everyone else. We are helplessly at odds:

> I have what you have not. I am what you are not. I have taken what you have failed to take and I have seized what you could never get. . . . And thus I spend my life admiring the distance between you and me; at times this even helps me to forget the other men who have what I have not and who have taken what I was too slow to take and who have seized what was beyond my reach . . . (NSC, 48).

Such a one has ceased to be real. One is lost in a "cult of pure illusion."

The I that makes these demands is not the true self at all. This "I" is incapable of regarding God or anyone else as a "Thou." It is incapable of loving, for all one can see is individuals in competition. "Perhaps even other people are merely extensions of the I, reflections of it, modifications of it, aspects of it" (CS, 1983, xviii, 4). The *cogito* has been given primacy and everything else must be rendered subordinate.

In contrast to this "superficial and empirical self" Merton would set the "true inner self, the true 'I'" that can love, but cannot reflect on itself (NSC, 279). The outer self can "have," "enjoy" and "accomplish," but in all of this it is only playing the role, or usurping the role, of the "person." This outer self is a person turned inside out; the "empirical ego" is the reality recognized by the world, while the true self is hidden in what the world regards as nothingness and void. "What we are not seems to be real, what we are seems to be unreal" (NSC, 281). To get away from this illusion one must reject the illusory self and with humility discover the "nothing" that comprises our true reality in God: "a point of nothingness which is un-touched by sin and by illusion" (CGB, 158). To know one's self as "nothing" can be disconcerting, for one seems to disappear altogether. Then one is left with freedom and the void—a free-dom indistinguishable from infinite Freedom. This freedom does not inhere in any human subject; "It is freedom living and circulating in God, Who is Freedom" (NSC, 284). Yet it is dis-tinct from God (Carr, SWS, 44).

The exterior ego had centered itself on pride, but the inner person can be found only in humility. Then the outer individ-ual vanishes like smoke and one can say of such a one:

> Here is a man who is dead and buried and gone and his memory has vanished from the world of men and he no longer exists among the living who wander about in time: and will you call him proud because the sunlight fills the huge arc of sky over the country where he lived and died and was buried, back in the days when he existed? So it is with one who has vanished into God by pure contemplation (NSC, 286).

Merton selected an appropriate scriptural text for his ordina-tion card: "He walked with God and was seen no more" (Gen 5:24). He wanted to think of his ego vanishing in a similar way.

Merton speculated that if ever one would vanish into God for the space of a minute, everything thereafter would be dif-ferent. Until then one's life might have been a welter of uncer-tainties and sins, but for one minute such a one is delivered into God; one's life has become pure and given pure glory to God. Only those who have known such a moment are capable of appreciating the world and the things in it, for they know the world is centered on God and not on themselves.

Though Merton would speak of the "complete annihilation of the ego," he allowed that some serious qualifications must be made and that the phrase could be misleading. But speaking this way makes it clear that *the ego can never be the subject of a "transcendent experience."* "The *person* which is the subject of this transcendent consciousness is not the ego as isolated and contingent, but the person as 'found' and 'actualized' in union with Christ" (Z, 75). The person here is a self which is "no-self." It is distinct from the Self of God and yet perfectly identified with him so that only a single Self appears. This is the "transcendent experience."

In calling this experience transcendent Merton wanted to make it clear that it has nothing to do with the ego. Others might call some type of ego experience mystical, but not Merton. Such experiences might indeed enhance the ego, but Merton insisted that such enhancement is not mysticism. For example, some people speak of mysticism in what could also be called psychological regression; there is a certain loss of identity as one slides into a warm, oceanic swoon. And even mystical literature can suggest such regression; he found this particularly true in Taoist mysticism and part of the Christian tradition (HGL, 493, 494). He allowed that "in a transitional and early phase of mystical development" there might be some regressive features. Those who identify regression with mysticism would never become mature. They would be "bogged down in this 'peace' and 'sweetness'" and refuse to make the leap into a "new being." Mystic union is not just a cosmic or oceanic feeling, for these involve no transcendence; they are only forms of heightened self-awareness. They are essentially narcissistic, for they allow the superficial, empirical, individualist ego to regard itself as the paradise of being. So a major task of any spiritual director is to help people "*not* to confuse this narcissistic self-awareness with true mystical contemplation." Earlier in the present Chapter it was argued that Merton had tried some such immersion into his monastic community. But he would later reject this as a "communal narcissism . . . centered in the self multiplied" (HGL, 495). One is still playing the Cartesian game in which the individual is the fundamental truth.

Merton would not allow that one can know the "transcendent" by taking drugs—as Aldous Huxley had proposed. He wrote to Huxley explaining the difference: the transcendent experience involved "a direct spiritual *contact of two liberties:*" divine Liberty and human liberty forming a personal relationship. This cannot be had from drugs. He explained to Huxley that in the transcendent experience

> God is known not as an "object" or as "him up there" or "him in everything" nor as "the All" but as—the biblical

expression—I AM, or simply, AM. . . . it is a presence of a
Person and *depends on the liberty of that Person* (HGL, 438;
italics in text).

Without the free act of the Other there is not mysticism. In
speaking of the "contact of two liberties," Merton is again saying that we find our person only "in relationship." Drugs bring
dependency, but the transcendent experience brings us a freedom from everything, except the grace of God (FV, 217).

Merton would likewise distinguish the transcendent experience from what some psychologists (Maslow, Fromm) have
termed a peak experience. Here one's ego feels itself to be at
the peak of its powers, but the experience is again centered
around the ego. Nor is the transcendent experience an aesthetic experience in which one seems to dwell above oneself
"in a heightening and intensification of our personal identity"
(R, 400). Nor is the transcendent experience the moral experience in which one rises above one's ordinary powers to per-
form a noble deed. Nor is it the rising out of ourselves into a
collective enthusiasm (NSC, 11). All such experiences might
leave us heightened and purified, yet they are not transcendent, for in each the self-aware subject remains self-aware.
While in the transcendent experience there is no subject left.

If the ego is still present, it can enrich itself, stretch itself,
and think better of itself. Then the ego can return to its familiar self and chalk up one more experience on its score card; the
"trip" it has taken has done wonders for increasing self esteem.
But, for Merton, if the ego were present at all, it would know itself to be "irrevelant, illusory, and indeed as the root of all ignorance." Should the empirical ego claim the transcendent
experience as its own, one would attain the "crowning glory of
egohood and self-fulfillment" (Z, 73). That is, the crowning
glory of illusion.

Today the Cartesian ego has impeded our ability to relate to
others and thus to pray: "the spirit of individualism, associated with the culture and economy of the West in the Modern
Age, has had a disastrous effect on the validity of Christian
prayer" (CP, 107). Today the individual tends to close in on
one's self and would like to remain that way "with more or less
permanent satisfaction" (CP, 107). This fixation on the self

produces reassurance and provides a sense of spiritual identity so that one need not face one's radical non-entity. This arrangement would work well were it not for dread. Dread draws us beyond the quiet idolatry of the "inner life" and into the mystery of God. But "we will dread His coming in proportion as we are identified with this exterior self and attached to it" (NSC, 15). It is therefore a grace when we find that the reflexive quality of our situation becomes a source of unrest and dissatisfaction (NMI, 47). Our consolations give way to fear and anguish as "we taste the awful dereliction of the soul closed in upon itself" (CP, 109). Dread is divesting us of the sense of "having" an objective being and all of the other defenses developed by the *cogito.* Dread brings us to face the radical defenselessness wherein we can do nothing but surrender to God in a desert of emptiness, but there the transcendent One reveals his unutterable mercy. In radical poverty we recognize that "individualist piety is then a poor substitute for true personalism" (CP, 109).

Merton believed that the transcendent experience is found in the Christian, the Buddhist, and the Sufi traditions. Christians speak of it when they tell of "having the mind of Christ," or of knowing another "in the Spirit of Christ." Other traditions would "call it Being, call it Atman, call it Pneuma . . . or Silence" (HGL, 15). But whatever the name, in order to come to the transcendent God, one must turn the ego-consciousness inside out so that we become a desert, a nothing, a void.

Buddhists would speak abundantly of emptying oneself and the void, and Merton identified with the Buddhists more than with any other religious tradition. But he would see a significant difference between himself and the Buddhist: the Buddhist has a transcendent ontological awareness, while the Christian has a transcendent awareness of a personal God. The person "is a value which seems to be totally missing from Buddhist thought" (Z, 118). (Yet, Merton wrote with delight of one Buddhist, named Nishida, who spoke of a personal God [ZBA, 67–70], but he knew this was not common in the Buddhist tradition.) Many have wondered why Merton felt such kinship with Buddhists and not with the Hindus who had a theism more like his own (see HGL, 499, 648). Part of the answer is that the Buddhists are "radical, austere and ruthless" in denying any reality to the ego-self. Without this radical stripping away of the ego in dread, there is no mysticism. Thus, Merton believed the *method* of the Buddhist should be the method of the Christian—even though the Christian would come to a theistic conclusion that the Buddhist would not. So Merton found Buddhism "very germane and close to our own *approaches* to inner truth in Christ" (HGL, 580).

Unless the ego-self disappears (the approach of Buddhism), Merton would not allow that a "transcendent experience" is possible. But when the ego disappears, what of the different conclusions of the Buddhist and the Christian? Merton allowed that Buddhism is more or less atheistic and even claimed "the majority of true mystics stand or fall with the existence of God" (HGL, 310). Then Buddhists would not seem to be mystics at all. This leaves some difficulty in trying to understand his appreciation of the Buddhists. Yet because he so identified with the Buddhist *approach,* he suggested that if the Buddhists did not allow the "person" in theory they did so in practice.

Merton would accept only the religious traditions which told of a radical self-emptying. For only these could be speaking of the "transcendent experience." Traditions that involve self-affirmation or self-fulfillment were dismissed, for they are concerned only with the individual affirming or improving one's ego. He believed these methods had deluded many, and he claimed that any competent spiritual director would be ruthless in opposing the attendant delusions of narcissism, spiritual ambition and self-complacency that these methods involved.

But it is difficult to say what this rejection would mean in practice. In his work as novice director Merton found many novices insecure and with little sense of their own identity (CAW, 77) while monastic training presumed novices "of strong character and powerful egos." So he would recommend that monasteries "ought to try to educate and develop them" (develop their character, their egos?) (SCh, 231). He warned that the psychological night "of facelessness, lack of identity," was not the same as the mystical night. That the monk should be kept "feeling useless, a non-entity," was said to be fatal today (SCh, 267). One can only conclude that for Merton there was a place for the development of one's ego identity emotionally and spiritually, an identity that would not simply feel "useless" and a no-one. (Though uselessness and non-self are integral to Zen and what he proposed.) This need of many novices for a very human development is the only way to understand Merton's introduction of culture (poetry, literature, etc.) into the training of novices—a practice that had not been common. He wanted the novices to have a basic self-confidence—together with a sense of having "no-self"! But in some way that tells of Merton himself: a confident and independent thinker who claimed he was a no-one.

How explain the paradox? Perhaps Merton was saying that one should have a social identity, a measure of social assurance, and be able to relate with others in an ordinary way. But this social self should also know an existential dread that radically undercuts all ego-illusions. Perhaps even a measure of social identity is necessary before one comes to the great questions of Being and one's own Nothingness.

This Chapter began by asking how a mystic involved in losing one's self could still be concerned with one's autobiography and day-by-day accounts of one's doings. Merton was always sensitive when others criticized him, his writings, what he taught the novices, or his own psychic balance. One would have to conclude that Merton the "individual" was alive and well, useful and industrious. Though he talked of disappearing in God, vanishing, annihilation and his own nothingness, he would add, "I am a joyful person. I like life" (CGB, 262). And he did.

2

Contemplation

Under the blunt pine
Elias becomes his own geography
(Supposing geography to be necessary at all),
Elias becomes his own wild bird,
with God in the center.

No term is more central to the thought of Thomas Merton than contemplation. But using the word in unexpected contexts he extended its meaning: the interior life of God is "perfect contemplation," and "Christ . . . came on earth to form contemplatives" (SC, 37, 156). Contemplation was the reason for human existence and the supreme goal of all theology (AT, 24, 76). Merton "defined" the term more than a hundred times, but the variety of his definitions—together with the ordinary difficulty in speaking of divine things—makes it impossible to state precisely what he meant. He has even warned against pseudo-scientific attempts to define contemplation (NSC, 6). In a general way, contemplation means the life of God active within a human subject. Merton would often quote St. Paul: "It is not I who live, but Christ who lives in me." This is contemplation.

Contemplation: *Metaphysical, Natural and Supernatural*

The best way to approach what Merton, and many others, meant by contemplation is to consider contemplation in analogy with the familiar experience of listening to an engaging speaker.

At such a time I seem to be lost in what I hear. So, Merton would often speak of contemplation as a listening: "Contemplation is essentially a listening in silence" (CP, 90). "What is the contemplative life if one does not listen to God in it?" (HGL, 79). "This is the contemplative life—listening to the Word, making our home in the Word, dwelling in the Word" (TMA, 76). We prepare for contemplation by the "attuning of the inmost heart to the voice of God" (VC, 188–189). Our role is "simply to consent, to listen" (R, 410). Merton spoke of his fellow monks "living as listeners," and of himself, "I came into solitude to hear the Word of God." In the simplicity of contemplation one becomes "absorbed in what is said to it, and (is) not aware of itself as existing outside of what is spoken to it" (HGL, 571).

When I am engrossed in listening (and also in reading), I seem to be lost to myself—my familiar identity has disappeared. That is, I might listen intently to an adventure story, but when it is over I cannot say that *I* have had an adventure, for all the time I listened, the "I" was suspended. To become involved my "I" had to disappear—and so it is with contemplation. To claim contemplation as one's own deed would stain "the pure emptiness where God's light shone." The contemplative finds it intolerable "to speak about it as his own experience" (SC, 174). Put in other terms: "Contemplation immolates our entire self to God" (AT, 13). "The first foundation of contemplation is to see you are nothing" (Life & Cont, tape).

In order to "lose myself" in listening, I must have *faith* in the speaker. If I am skeptical, I hold back and my "I" does not disappear. So Merton claimed, "faith is the first step towards contemplation" (AT, 254; NSC, 126). But faith continues through all that follows; one travels purely by faith. When listening to the word of another, sense knowledge has been set aside. So in contemplation "the old world of our senses . . . seems to us strange, remote and unbelievable" (NSC, 226). Thus, in both intense listening and contemplation, we can forget our immediate surroundings, forget our feelings of hunger and the fact that the room might be cold, for we have been drawn apart from the world of sense. So in contemplation there is a "darkening" of sense; God comes as "darkness to my experience"

(SC, 29).[7] "Contemplation means rest, suspension of activity" (SSM, 410). The analogy with reading could explain. While listening to an engaging speaker, we can feel passive yet active. Absorbed in what we hear, we seem to be finding a whole new world, but it is given to us; we do not have to evaluate it or think about it for ourselves. Another seems to be thinking within us and for us. In listening intently to a story, our own mind does not need to interpret what it hears; this is done by a trusted authority who tells us all that we need to know. There is activity in our mind, but we are not doing it—we are passive, we are receptive. A similar sense of receptive passivity, of another acting within us, is integral to contemplation. "One is grabbed by God" (Cont&Renun, tape). Yet it is an "active passivity" (NSC, 86). It is not simply a matter of no action at all; God acts in us and for us. The contemplative even feels unable to act.

While absorbed in listening to another, we can even feel "glued to our chair," unable to move or act on our own. So in contemplation "the activity of the faculties is at least to some extent impeded by the action of God" (AT, 230). Contemplation "holds us by some obscure but inexplicable charm. It captivates us. It keeps us prisoners. It will not allow us to escape from the hidden power that works on the depths of our spirit" (AT, 209). In contemplation "one is powerless to do anything for one's self" (CS, 1984, xix, 64). Thus in both contemplation and intense listening we are passive; in both there is an activity within us that is not ours; on our own we feel unable to act.

But beyond losing ourselves in *what* we hear, we can sometimes go further and identify with *who* we hear. In the first case the matter presented occupies all our attention; we seem to lose ourself into what we are told. So in contemplation we know truth "not so much by seeing it as by being absorbed into it" (SC, 134). But at certain times we can pass beyond the matter expressed and find we identify with the speaker. We sense the other active within us and this so absorbs our attention

---

[7]This disappearance of the sense world in contemplation could best explain the apocalyptic imagery that runs through his early writing. See *Figures for an Apocalypse,* "The Fire Watch," and especially *My Argument with the Gestapo* (35, 74, 235, 244, 253, 255). In *Enchantments* I have argued this radical destruction of the world is associated with the power of God's word (E, 146ff.).

that we might pay little account to what is being said. We seem to know what the other knows and desire what the other desires. We might say that the other lives within us; but we could just as well say that we are living in the other. So in contemplation we might say God lives within us, or just as well say we live in God. The subjectivity of Another has replaced our own. We are no longer facing God as an object; we are united with God in the "transcendent subjectivity" of love; we have lost ourselves in him (R, 409). We are "in some way transformed into him, so that we know him as he knows himself" (SC, 74). He is knowing within us. "God and the soul seem to have but one single 'I.' They are (by divine grace) as though one single person" (CS, 1983, vol xviii, 15). The Greek Fathers spoke of "divinization" and Merton accepted the term (AT, 15–16).

Thus, on one level we can identify with what is said—but on a deeper level with *who* is speaking. This identification with the subjectivity of another is a way of understanding the numerous references to love that abound in Merton's accounts of contemplation. For Merton love always involves passing out of ourself to identify with another:

> All love tends to ecstasy, in the sense that it takes us out of ourselves and makes us live in the object of our love. In the case of human love, this ecstasy can never be more than a figure of speech, or a mere matter of moral and psychological agreement. But since our souls are spiritual substances and since God is pure Spirit, there is nothing to prevent a union between ourselves and Him that is ecstatic in the literal sense of the word (AT, 280).

Again, the loving identification can be understood through reference to the analogy with listening. I can seem to identify with the beloved who speaks, but it is only a matter of "seeming." It is not so with God: the ecstatic identification with the other takes place "in the literal sense of the word."

For Merton there are two types of contemplation: natural and supernatural. The first is called active contemplation or *theoria physika;* and the second is called passive or infused contemplation or *theologia.* Only the second is contemplation in the full and proper sense, and only the second is identified as mysticism. The two forms of contemplation will be shown to parallel the two forms of listening presented above. The first will be a loving identification with *what* is said and may even include a loving consideration of the speaker as a beloved object; the second will involve a radical identification with the speaker as a transcendent subject. One seems to be the speaker. In the second there is an ecstasy in which we have passed out of ourselves and "become" the Other.

But the types of contemplation in Merton are not that simple, for Merton has presented *two* forms of natural contemplation. The first is called a "metaphysical intuition." It occurs apart from any revealed text. This was considered in the previous section where it was identified as the starting point for philosophy and set in opposition to the Cartesian *cogito*. This intuition would maintain that "the basic reality is being itself, which is one in all concrete existents, which shares itself among them and manifests itself through them" (HR, 89).

Thus, in a truer sense, there are three types of contemplation in Merton (two natural and one infused). But there would seem to be only a single text in which Merton spoke of them as three: he said the contemplative life "can be considered from three points of view, as it were in three degrees" (FA, 95). The first is that of the artist and the philosopher; the second is that of the Christian trying to dispose one's self for union with God; and the third is mystical union with God.

Merton himself would associate the first type of contemplation with Zen, though his own consideration of this contemplation contained many elements that Zen did not (these differences were considered above). Merton considered this contemplation to be the fundamental awareness that we should have as human beings. But we have become so taken up with appearances that we no longer see the world as it is. Most people cannot even grasp the abstract notions of being and goodness as proposed by philosophers. They think only in terms of concrete and particular beings. They see signs showing healthy folk consuming cold beer and driving shiny cars, and this rates as "Being" or "Goodness" (AT, 196). However, when one frees oneself from this preoccupation with material things and one's natural capacities are restored, one begins to taste what properly belongs to the human soul: the metaphysical intuition, natural contemplation.

Merton saw people desiring the Good, but they have been led to believe they can attain it by consumption. They want to possess all goodness as their own. But their attempts at gaining being by consumption will never work; they are condemning themselves to frustration. On one level they know they soon will be frustrated, but they behave as if they thought otherwise. But Merton believed their desire to share in all goodness need not be frustrated, for

> . . . all the reality that exists, and all the goodness of every-
> thing that exists and is good, can be spiritually tasted and en-
> joyed in a single metaphysical intuition of being and of
> goodness as such. The clean intellectual delight of such an
> experience makes all the inebriation produced by wine look
> like a hangover. I am not now talking of anything mystical:
> merely of the natural intuition of pure being, pure goodness.
> Here the being and goodness which are shared by all particu-
> lar things are grasped in a single luminous intuition which
> floods our whole spirit with light and exhilaration (AT, 197).

Merton would call this a kind of natural ecstasy in which our being recognizes in itself a kinship with all being. We rise above all the particulars "to discover all things in one undifferentiated transcendental reality, which is being itself." This is not an abstraction to which we might argue; it is "not an abstract objective idea but a fundamental concrete intuition directly apprehended in a personal experience that is incontrovertible and inexpressible" (Z, 26). This intuition should be natural to the human condition.

In this intuition we see the value of creation and of our own personal depths. We have found the deep substantial reality of our own being, and this turns out to be far different from what is found in the *cogito*. We know ourselves as persons, and at the same time we pass beyond our persons to "an intuition of the Absolute Being." This is not yet an immediate intuition of God. At this stage God is still realized by inference from created being; he is known as reflected in ourselves and in the things he has made. God is known as "present in the metaphysical depths of everything that is," but he is not known "in His infinite transcendence" (BW, 43). To know him in his transcendence, God must reveal himself directly and not only in his works.

This metaphysical intuition can even involve an intuitive *appreciation* of God. This intuition is tinged with affectivity; the creature is filled with vitality, joy, and even love. This experience is so intense that pagan philosophers considered it our highest beatitude, but it is only the highest beatitude that one can attain by one's natural powers (see, however, CS, 1983, xviii, 298). Though one could attain this appreciation by one's human powers, Merton believed that most of those who attain this awareness do so by supernatural grace. Yet the intuition itself is natural. This would seem to be the contemplation of which Merton was writing in most of the opening passages of *The New Seeds of Contemplation*. And this would be the contemplation of which Merton would speak abundantly in his later writing. Merton would claim this natural intuition is the starting point for Christian belief and experience. It already has its own religious quality, but Christian belief takes one beyond this. The classic experience of the Christian mystics "is rooted in a metaphysic of being, in which God is intuited as 'He Who Is,' as the supreme reality, pure Being" (Z, 28). Yet this intuition is not infused contemplation; it is only the metaphysical ground in which the experience of the Christian mystic is rooted. Each time Merton told of this experience, he insisted that it was nonreflective. And in telling of the experience God was identified as Being, IS, I am, or as Source (CS, 1983, xviii, 9).

Merton was aware that many Christians today reject the "metaphysical" or "Hellenic" philosophy that undergirds this intuition. He was also aware that many contemporary philosophers had turned away from classical forms (Z, 30; MZM, 205). But he did not see anything in phenomenology that could replace this intuition—phenomenology is a contemporary philosophy that relies heavily on the Cartesian *cogito*. He found many Christians dismissing this metaphysical intuition—or modifications of it—to claim that God is known only as a summons to action. These Christians would become lost in social reform and "community building" and deny the need for any philosophy. He did not agree with them. He believed that a basic metaphysical intuition must ground the Christian life. Yet he expressed a limited willingness to give the matter further consideration (see Z, 30).

In this presentation of the metaphysical intuition, the analogy of "listening" might seem to have been forgotten. But its relevance can be seen in the way Merton picked up on scriptural references that speak of all things being created in Christ: thus all things express the divine Word that God had spoken in them. Things are what they have been told to be by God, and God still speaks in them. Those able to hear the word of God in nature would be attuned to "the inner spiritual reality (the *logos*) of the created thing" (R, 408; parenthesis in text). So the metaphysical intuition comes from listening to God in nature rather than from our own activity. More significant applications of the analogy with listening will be evident in the material that follows.

In the early works of Merton this metaphysical intuition was considered only briefly, but perhaps due to his increased involvement in ecumenical work, it became increasingly important. The metaphysical intuition provided a better basis for dialogue with Eastern monks than a contemplation entirely centered on the Judaeo-Christian revelation. He would explain how the two interrelate:

> . . . the supernatural Kerygma and the metaphysical intuition of the ground of being are far from being incompatible. One may be said to prepare the way for the other. They can well complement each other, and for this reason Zen is perfectly compatible with Christian belief and indeed with Christian mysticism (if we understand Zen in its pure state, as metaphysical intuition) (Z, 47; parenthesis in text).

It is clear that Merton himself found the metaphysical intuition and the Christian faith compatible. It was through reading Gilson's book *The Spirit of Mediaeval Philosophy* that he first came to recognize the existence of God. While reading Gilson Merton was fascinated by the Latin philosophical term "*Aseitas*": God was pure Being and in no way dependent on any other Being. His conversion began with a philosophical term. He noted on the page: "Aseity of God—God is Being *per se*." He went through the book marking other passages: "He is the pure act of existence." He felt a "profound satisfaction"

with what he read, for by his reading he felt God was vindicated. Reading Gilson enabled Merton to see that knowledge
of God was possible. This was in February 1937, before he seriously considered entering the Church. His Christian faith
would later "complement" this intuition, but it would not sup-
plant it. His regard for philosophy and the metaphysical intuition remained throughout his life. He argued this awareness
was not the property of any one religion; it is the foundation of
all natural religion. It is "a natural preamble to supernatural
faith" (R, 393). He would often tell of both of them in sequence: first the metaphysical and then the supernatural (BW,
43; HR, 89; AT, 205; R, 409).

On the night before his death in Bangkok, Merton said to a
friend: "Zen and Christianity are the future" (Moffitt, 275).
"Zen" would refer to this metaphysical intuition of Being.
Merton saw this essential to the future world and he could not
envision a Christian mysticism lacking this foundation. Again,
the natural knowing was listed first (Zen and Christianity). In
his early writing Merton concentrated on the revelation he
found in Scripture and Church teaching. But in coming to
speak more with his own voice, this metaphysical intuition became more important. He came to believe that the other
monks needed, beyond their Christian devotion, a greater
grounding in *theoria physika,* and by this term from the Greek
Fathers Merton was referring to the natural intuition.

In coming to Christian faith, Merton found his natural desire to know God was confirmed and extended. He was absorbed into the revealed texts and then into the Speaker to
Whom he listened so intently. But this required more than philosophy. "The passage from philosophical understanding to
faith is marked by a gift of our self to God. The moment of
transition is the moment of sacrifice" (AT, 116). By faith we
pass beyond the metaphysical intuition that we have more or
less on our own to accept what God has told us. We study the
revelation and find that its message brings us delight, peace
and joy, but this is still natural contemplation. It is natural for
it is we who direct our thoughts and imagination to God as we
consider Him serenely and *objectively.* The soul is active and
functions in a familiar way: it reasons, imagines, and makes
acts of the will. It is active. It considers what it knows from

Scripture, theology, and philosophy and through these directs a simple and affective gaze upon God. Music, the arts, and especially the liturgy can help us focus our attention. By concentration one is able to regard God with simplicity and reverence (WC, 12). Though we are resting in a gaze on what we know through revelation, and though we are somewhat passive; it is still "active" contemplation.

Merton judged some active contemplation to be absolutely essential for the Christian life.[8] Still those with natural contemplation are only quasi-contemplatives. For the entirety of their contemplation is within the created universe. "To rest in the beauty of God as a pure concept . . . is a pleasure which still belongs to the natural order" (SC, 124). Through such an awareness one can come to the prayer of repose, but it remains "just as much a created thing as a glass of beer" (SC, 120).

In natural contemplation we still know ourselves as subjects having an experience of the divine Presence. In a vague and ill-defined way, we want more. We seek more than the created order can give, but we cannot identify what this is or know how to attain it. To fulfill our yearning we must pass beyond all that is created to God himself. We must pass from the *what* to the *Who*.

In supernatural contemplation God freely renders himself present. His coming is not the result of a natural process or discipline on our part. We can make a radical self-immolation; then, on some occasions, God becomes present where our self had been (AT, 116). But the deciding factor "is the free and unpredictable action of God" (CS, 1984, xix, 63). His unpredictable action effects our divinization: God is living within us—or better still it is "God living in God" (SC, 186). "I live, now no longer I, but Christ lives in me." There is no self awareness. This is not a knowledge of God in his creatures, for no creature is involved. This is God living in his eternal Word, or God liv-

---

[8]In his early writings Merton had seen infused contemplation as that to which all the baptized were called (WC, 5; FA, 96), though he allowed that many because of their temperament or situation in life were presently incapable of it. He would come to speak of it as the lot of very few (AT, 8; see CP, 115; CS, 1983, xviii, 294–95). After dealing with many young monks, he said: "I do not think strictly that contemplation should be the goal of 'all devout souls,' though I may have said this earlier on" (HGL, 345). Others were called to a different spirituality (NSC, xi).

ing in God; it is God's eternal contemplation of himself. "HE IS—and this reality absorbs everything else" (NSC, 267).

Consider again the basic analogue: listening. As there are two kinds of contemplation, so there are two ways we can be absorbed in listening. We can become absorbed in what another is saying: the matter occupies our attention. But sometimes we seem to pass out of ourselves altogether. The mind of the other seems to be our mind, and we are lost in a loving identification. The subjectivity of the other seems to have replaced our own. Now all objectivity is gone. God is known as the deeper subject within.

In listening to the word of God, Merton saw particular importance in the words of divine revelation. He lost himself in the texts of Christianity and even insisted that a contemplative must be formed "with doctrinal pronouncements and disciplinary degrees" (BW, 28, 41; see SC, 81). He argued that mysticism is based on dogma, and not, as often suggested, dogma based on mysticism (see AT, 243ff.). He was so sure that some inspired teaching is integral to mysticism that he allowed that Eastern mystics must have had some revelation (AT, 67; HGL, 470). Therefore, the leading holy ones in Islam, Hinduism, and Buddhism "*could* have been mystics in the true supernatural sense" (MZM, 207). He first made these claims with little familiarity with the sacred texts of the East, though later he gained a considerable familiarity with them. He was arguing *a priori* from the fact that his own mysticism was centered on listening to the revealed words. Merton seems to believe that the act of listening to divine revelation is more important than the content revealed—much like one can enjoy the presence of another without much regard for what is being said.

Supernatural or infused contemplation begins when the direct intervention of God raises the human process above the human level. Then one becomes part of the act of pure love by which God knows himself; one says in amazement, "God's reality lives within me" (SC, 122, 18). Then "our contemplation of him is a participation of his contemplation of himself" (SC, 16). The activities of our own life have been suspended. We are completely above our nature, yet it seems "'normal' and 'natural' to see as we now see without seeing." We have "entered a depth that leaves us wholly inarticulate" (SC, 135). We have

above our nature = contemplation

"an immediate grasp of God's substance" (R, 405). Now the Truth is present "without the medium of created concept;" Truth has ceased being "a body of abstractions and becomes a living reality which is God himself" (SC, 75). One is actually sharing "though in a dark and inchoate manner, in the contemplation by which God knows and loves His own Divine Essense" (AT, 253). Selfhood has been left behind: "Contemplation immolates our entire self to God" (AT, 13). The action of senses, imagination, or the discoursing mind have nothing to do with infused contemplation. We are delivered

> from images and concepts, from the forms and shadows of all the things men desire with human appetites. It brings deliverance from the feeble and delusive analogies we ordinarily use to arrive at God.

Merton has described the coming of infused contemplation with eloquent simplicity:

> A door opens in the center of our being and we seem to fall through it into immense depths which, although they are infinite, are all accessible to us; all eternity seems to have become ours in this one placid and breathless contact. God touches us with a touch that is emptiness and empties us. He moves us with a simplicity that simplifies us. All variety, all complexity, all paradox, all multiplicity cease. Our mind swims in the air of an understanding, a reality that is dark and serene and includes in itself everything. Nothing more is desired. . . . You feel as if you were at last fully born. All that went before was a mistake, a fumbling preparation for birth. . . . And yet now you have become nothing. You have sunk to the center of your own poverty, and there you have felt the doors fly open into infinite freedom, into a wealth that is perfect because none of it is yours and yet it all belongs to you (SC, 139–140).

Though sometimes Merton will speak of infused contemplation as an *experience* ("mystical contemplation . . . is first of all a supernatural experience of God" [AT, 16]), he would generally claim it is not an experience at all, for an experience implies there is a subject who has the experience ("experience has to be experienced by someone") (SC, 185). But during the time of infused contemplation the human subject is "immolated" and seems to have vanished. Merton would accordingly speak of the soul becoming nothing, being "annihilated," in its union with God (AT, 75–76). Infused contemplation is God rejoicing in his own liberty. It is "God living in God and identifying a created life with his own Life" (SC, 186). The mind of God is living where our mind had been. Afterwards we might call it an experience. But even then it would be intolerable to speak of it as one's own. St. Paul wrote of "his" contemplation as though it had happened to another: "I know a man who was taken up to the third heaven. . . ."

Though Merton rarely wrote about his own prayer, the one extended account that he left tells of a self-annihilation.

> Strictly speaking I have a very simple way of prayer. It is centered entirely on attention to the presence of God and to His will and His love. That is to say that it is centered on *faith* by which alone we can know the presence of God. . . . it is a matter of adoring him as invisible and infinitely beyond our comprehension, and realizing him as all. . . . My prayer is then a kind of praise rising up out of the center of Nothing and Silence. If I am still present "myself" this I recognize as an obstacle about which I can do nothing unless he himself removes the obstacle. If he wills he can then make the Nothingness into a total clarity (HGL, 63–64).

Prayer depends on God's will: the result is not automatic. His presence cannot be achieved by method or determination: "No effort will make us mystics." And the presence of God can be simply stated in the divine "I am," or simply "AM"—thus God revealed himself to Moses and thus he reveals himself to the mystic. God is not present as an object. He is present as the unnameable "I am"—a phrase Merton repeatedly used when telling of the height of the mystical experience (R, 402; NSC, 4, 9, 13; Z, 26; CS, 1983, xviii, 9). Contemplation realizes there "is no such thing as God," for God is a pure *Who*. Merton would speak of contemplation as love. For we are involved in a subjectivity that is other than our own. Then we "see Him in ourselves by losing ourselves in Him" (R, 409).

This is the contemplation that Christ came to bring us, the fullness of the Christian vocation. It is the foretaste of eternal joy. St. Thomas called contemplation the "*inchoatio vitae aeternae.*" We are fundamentally passive, yet we are the "place" of an intense activity. God is the doer. Our own activity would be an obstacle to what God is infusing within us. We must not interrupt "with arguments or words, conceptions or activities that belong to the level of our own tedious and labored existence" (NSC, 230). We are poised in silent acceptance unable to increase or retain the divine Presence. It is pure gift. When contemplation is over we fall back into our own selfhood. But "we carry a scar" over the place where contemplation had exalted in our hearts. We weep for the day this Presence will hold us again and never let us go.

In contemplation our senses with their images and our mind with its ambitions and judgments are set aside; we are relieved of the whole burden of opinions by which we identify ourselves. Merton will often speak of contemplation in terms of a "darkness," an "emptiness" and a "sacrifice;" for human faculties of thinking and sensing have been "darkened" and "emptied" by the divine Presence, and "no emptiness is empty enough" (SC, 168). Our human faculties have been "sacrificed" so that the divine Light may occupy us. To reintroduce the analogy of listening: we seem to disappear as ourselves when we are engrossed in listening to another.

This section has told of three forms of contemplation in the texts of Merton: the metaphysical, the natural, and the infused. Only the second of these (a natural contemplation) still involves a subject looking at an object and Merton was reluctant to call this contemplation at all: "the whole essence of contemplative prayer is that the division between subject and object disappears" (TMA, 144). Both the first (metaphysical contemplation) and the third (infused contemplation) which is mysticism properly speaking, deny the whole subject-looking-at-object system. And in Merton's writings on contemplation there seems to be no point that Merton insisted on more consistently (R, 411, 483; MZM, 214, 245; CS, 1983, xviii, 122; CS, 1984, xix, 69). Both the metaphysical and the infused contemplation reject the Cartesian ego which *has* an experience of itself and of the world. And both as nonreflective pass beyond "consciousness *of*" to identify with Being itself.

But still there are fundamental differences between the two. A metaphysical intuition does not put us into contact with God as he is in himself, but only God as he is in his creatures; while infused contemplation gives us God as he is in himself and no creature is involved. Another difference is that the metaphysical intuition is not based on any revealed teaching; it depends only on immediate experience. The metaphysical intuition leads to a content that the contemplative can state, and Merton stated it often (see his letter on contemplation where he offered conclusions for which "only experience counts" [MJ, 220]). That is, metaphysical contemplation will lead the contemplative to a teaching that he or she can state in words. But infused contemplation is the reverse: it must begin with a teaching and from there proceed to the mystical state. Unlike metaphysical contemplation, infused contemplation would seem to lead to no conclusion.

The previous chapter considered at length Merton's effort at losing himself. He found that the busy activity of his mind planning books and essays hindered the receptivity needed for contemplation. The very process of forming his own judgments continually affirmed the "point of view" by which he maintained his own identity. This distinctive sense of self (and the importance any author attaches to his text) renders contemplation difficult. Accordingly, Merton would speak of the peasant as best suited for contemplation, for (Merton believed) the peasant would not have a strong sense for the importance of his own judgments. The anonymous pamphlets sold at the monastery ("A Trappist advises. . . .") seemed to be written by any one and no one; the author was stating only the point of view that was common at the monastery; it was not particularly his. In being detached from one's own thoughts one could be more disposed to contemplation than if one adopted a distinctive point of view. In uniting with God the mystic has become no one.

> Here is a man who is dead and buried and gone and his memory has vanished from the world of men and he no longer exists among the living who crawl about in time. . . . So it is with one who has vanished into God by pure contem-

plation. God alone is left. He is the identity that acts there. He is the one that loves and knows and rejoices (SC, 188).

The simple soul is like soft wax, while those with a distinctive identity can be harsh and brittle; those with published opinions are committed to defend them. The soft wax is best able to receive the divine stamp.

Though Merton had personal difficulties with religious obedience, he continued to defend it. The obedient person does not assert one's own will but "is nourished by obedience" (SC, 169). The contemplative has "a hunger to be led and advised and directed by somebody else;" the contemplative has "a passion for obedience" (SC, 106). This passion is associated with the desire to lose one's self in the words and identity of another. This involvement with obedience would not seem to describe the metaphysical contemplation that requires no verbal revelation.

Merton would refer to contemplatives as the little ones, the humble ones that the world ignores, but in their obscurity they are in union with God. Powerful ones are too weak for the joy of contemplation. The contemplative knows as God knows and all things are present to the divine Mind, so the contemplatives are able to enjoy life. By their humility, their poverty, and their limited sense of self, they are ignored by the busy and influential people of the world. But the world is theirs. "Blessed are the meek, for they shall possess the land."

The Mystic and the Intellect

The contemplation presented in *The Seeds of Contemplation* involved a radical denial of the human world:

> For the way to God lies through deep darkness in which all knowledge and all created wisdom and all pleasure and prudence and all human hope and human joy are defeated and annulled by the overwhelming purity of the light and the presence of God. Nothing that we can know and nothing that we can enjoy and desire with our natural faculties can be anything but an obstacle to the pure possession of Him as He is in Himself . . . (SC, 123).

The human seemed to disappear; it was not so much God acting in a human subject as the annihilation of the human subject and only "God living in God" (SC, 186). This seeming annihilation can explain the "scouring" of the soul that Merton saw integral to the monastic life (see chapter I).

But many Christians would have problems with Merton's claim: if "nothing that we can know" can be other than an obstacle to union with God, does this include the Christian creed?—a teaching we can more or less know. If a radical scouring of the soul prepares one for contemplation, what does the scouring do to our humanity? And, if God is really so transcendent, would human actions, thoughts, loves and desires make any difference with God at all?

In December 1948 Merton began writing a book to deal with these issues. It would eventually be called *The Ascent to Truth* and would consider "the prelude of mysticism" (AT, 288), rather than mysticism (infused contemplation) itself.[9] But in trying to resolve these problems Merton encountered more than his usual difficulties with writing: in February 1949 he claimed, "My work has been tied up in knots for two months." He set the work aside and picked it up in April to write, "I sit at the typewriter, with my fingers all wound up in a cat's cradle of strings." He had filled more than eight hundred notebook pages of material only to find an "unthinkable thing," a "hidden volcano" erupting within (SJ, 226). Only cryptic phrases tell of his difficulty, but he seems to have been dealing personally with the issues of which he would write. Having said contemplation required the vanishing of the historical self, he found himself weakened by feelings of his own "nonexistence." He spoke of a "writer's block" and then composed fifty pages only to tear them up and write additional pages he did not like. But after being unable to act for a year and a half, he found a new source of energy and finished the work. A large part of this book is an academic study of the scholastic tradition, but much of it is personal. The mixture is sometimes con-

---

[9]Merton would later call this his "emptiest" book. The prose is often difficult and shows the strain the author was going through at the time. Here it is considered at length, for by the labor of writing the book Merton resolved many personal issues. An earlier work had related prayer and the understanding (WAW, 11ff.).

fusing. The book is often repetitious and bears evidence of the difficulties Merton had while writing it.

In *The Ascent to Truth* Merton rejected the common assumption that mysticism had nothing to do with the intellect. This assumption would see the mystic opposed to all dogma. Since mystics have directly experienced truth, would not they be independent of both philosophy and theology? But Merton insisted that true mysticism is based on dogma and is "always essentially intelligent" (AT, 91, 13). He allowed that many mystics have spoken of an unknowing or an ignorance, but claimed this ignorance is not a rejection of intelligence, it is an appeal to a higher form of intelligence (AT, 59). Contemplation does not occur independent of knowledge, for it must be based on "speculative theology and philosophy" (AT, 87). Fundamentally *The Ascent to Truth* is Merton's attempt to explain the primacy of the intellect in the act of contemplation. Contemplation is the intellect's ascent to Truth; for contemplation is a *simplex intuitus veritatis* (AT, 205).

Merton believed that any mystic must face a fundamental dilemma: if mysticism does not include some noetic content, the intellect would not be involved. And, if the intellect is not involved, mysticism would leave the mystic divided against one's self (the heart would be involved and not the mind)—and inner division is the sign of false mysticism. But, on the other hand, if the mysticism does involve some noetic content, the infinite God would be known by a finite intelligence. One is caught on the horns of a *philosophical* dilemma. One seems to be lost in either alternative, for in the mystical act one must know and not know. Merton tried to steer a middle course between these alternatives by insisting that true mysticism is centered on faith. In faith one knows and does not know. Many Christians are at peace with the ambiguous nature of faith, but Merton claimed that one called to infused contemplation finds this ambiguity leads to a crisis within crisis, an anguish within anguish. For faith makes use of concepts, yet it tells of more than concepts can contain. Faith "sees God, but only in darkness, *per speculum, in aenigmate.* To see in darkness is not to see. To understand in an enigma is not to understand but to be perplexed" (AT, 107). Then Merton adds that the cross is the only way to mystical prayer. And the cross is not for the body and appetites alone; it is primarily for the intellect.

In *The Ascent* Merton takes pains to identify with a Catholic intellectual tradition that runs from St. Thomas Aquinas, St. Teresa, St. John of the Cross, and on to the contemporary scholastics Jacques and Raissa Maritain. It sometimes seemed Merton wanted to lose his own voice in this highly orthodox line of Catholic mysticism, much as he had tried to lose his own voice in his monastic community. Merton continued to claim that "contemplation immolates our entire self to God," but the overall concern of *The Ascent* was to show that nonetheless the intellect plays an important part in the process (AT, 13–14). He insisted on the importance of a teaching for the mystic; he quoted Pope Pius XII to the effect that there is a perfect conformity between theological science and mystical contemplation: people are not sanctified "by destroying their humanity" (AT, 16). But such statements only point up the dilemma.

Having appealed to authority, Merton tried to take a middle course between the claim that one can attain contemplation by one's own intellect and the counter claim that contemplation ignores the intellect altogether. The first alternative would lead to rationalism and the second to agnosticism. The first would involve one in a pharisaism of knowledge proud of the understanding one has acquired, while the second would involve one in a pharasaism of ignorance with feelings of complacent superiority to all learning. The first would reduce God to the size of human knowing, and the second would divide the human being against oneself by excluding the intellect.

Merton saw the Oriental mystic guilty of the rationalistic excess. Oriental mysticism was said to be "far more intellectual and speculative than the mysticism of the West, and this is, in fact, one of its deficiencies. It is *too* intellectual" (AT, 67). He saw Eastern mysticism depending almost exclusively on human intelligence with little room for love or the action of grace. It is not clear which Oriental mystics Merton had in mind, but his critique could apply best to Shankara and some forms of Vedanta.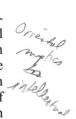

But in contrast to this, Merton claimed that the West is now attracted by the anti-intellectual, anti-rational form of mysticism. This would urge one to

> . . . throw his spirit into the hands of some blind life-force, considered sometimes as beyond man, sometimes as within himself. Sometimes this mysticism is political, sometimes religious. It almost always exalts emotion above thought, and its reply to intellectual argument is sometimes a program of systematic violence—the suppression of schools, the destruction of books, and the imprisonment of learned men. Why all this? Because the intelligence itself is regarded with suspicion (AT, 60–61).

According to this anti-intellectual ideal, reason must be renounced in order that "more vital" mystical impulses may find expression. Merton found this false mysticism in numerous writers of the present time; while in earlier times the Romantic revival had made a mystic of anyone with a sense of unutterable *Weltschmertz.* But there have also been anti-rational mysticisms within the Christian tradition. Merton told of Quietists who claimed that anyone learned in theology was ill equipped to be a mystic. The Quietists saw little importance in revelation and rejected all theology. Their error concerned Merton in a special way as it had a superficial resemblance to what St. John of the Cross was saying when he told of darkening the intellect. But, though John of the Cross was constantly talking of darkening the intellect, Merton insisted he was not irrational or anti-intellectual (AT, 56).

Within the Church Merton found two orthodox traditions; these would turn out to be modified forms of the above two heresies. There is a *via positiva,* a theology and mysticism of light that would emphasize the knowability of God. He saw this tradition exemplified in St. Augustine, St. Bernard, and St. Thomas. And there is a *via negativa,* a theology and mysticism of darkness emphasizing the hiddenness of God. Merton saw this tradition exemplified in St. Gregory of Nyssa, Pseudo-Dionysius, and St. John of the Cross. The first is a way of affirmation and the second a way of negation. But both traditions contain a balanced use of the intellect that avoids the two extremes of rationalism and agnosticism. Merton spoke of the two orthodox mysticisms as two lanes of the same highway that is leading to transcendent Truth (AT, 100).

Both the *via positiva* and the *via negativa* recognize there is a problem in claiming one has a human knowledge of God: human knowledge concerns what is limited and defined, while God is beyond all limits and definitions. Therefore, to speak of God one must begin by affirming something of God; e.g.: God is just. But we cannot mean this in the same sense in which we say that a human being is just. Our human concepts cannot literally apply to God at all.[10] So the theologians of darkness spoke of the way to God as a systematic denial of any human concepts. Merton compared this to the sculptor who makes progress by cutting away the stone. In the *via negativa* one is continually saying, "This is not God. This is not God." The intellect arrives at God only by negating all that one knows. The final result can be stated only in the form of paradox: We have "dark knowledge" of God, or "learned ignorance," or *Deus cognoscitur tamquam ignotum* (God is known as unknown). This is the way God is identified in the way of negation. But there still remains some sense in which the human mind truly knows God. It knows by not knowing, so that neither the darkness of agnosticism nor the light of rationalism can contain the full truth. Paradox tells of the situation: God reveals himself as hidden; he is known as unknown; he is the darkness which is light, the nothing that is all, the emptiness that is full. But even though one is able to speak only in paradox, paradox is recognized by the intellect. The intellect is involved.

In *The Ascent to Truth* Merton wrote a somewhat detailed study of the scholastic tradition that maintained contemplation is the act of the intellect and not of the will.[11] At times he seemed caught in doubletalk when speaking of the role of each of these faculties.[12] But he was following a carefully worked out

[10]This could be seen in St. Augustine. St. Augustine spoke of God abundantly (always active and always at rest, etc.). But then he asked, "What have I said? . . . What can any man succeed in saying when he tries to speak of you, when even those who know most can say nothing?" (*Confessions*, I, 3). This is apophatic theology; one begins by speaking of God, but then one adds that one can say nothing of Him. Meister Eckhart would have it, "Only the hand that erases can write the true thing."

[11]A later text speaking of mystical contemplation would claim that "on its higher level it transcends the intellect itself" (CS, 1984, xix, 63).

[12]Consider the following texts: "For God makes himself immediately present to the contemplative soul not by knowledge but by love. Thus, from the very first, love plays a preeminently important role in contemplation, even though contemplation

tradition that differed from the tradition of St. Augustine, who told of the primacy of the will in contemplation. Both Augustine and the scholastics regarded contemplation as the highest human activity (a tradition with roots in Plato and Aristotle). As the highest human activity it must involve the highest faculty: for the Augustinian this was the will and for the Thomist the intellect. Merton would follow the Thomists (AT, 194, 274, 314).

Both the Augustinian and the Thomist believed that when the highest faculty is functioning properly, one has attained that for which one was made; and both traditions believed the human was made for contemplation. When the highest faculty is properly functioning, it was understood that all the rest of the personality would fall into place. So each tradition tried to identify the highest human faculty, that whose functioning would unify the person. Though Merton claimed this faculty to be the intellect, he believed the will generally attains God before the intellect. When the will has found God, one feels great love for God. It can seem that the other faculties are uniting around this love, but Merton believed this is not necessarily the case. The intellect can still stand free.

Merton, following St. Thomas, insisted that the will is blind and of itself is not able to identify what is moving it. The will might become lost in an unidentified rapture, while the mind knows better. The result is a division of the person; the will is being moved by God, but the intellect has been violated or ignored. The will feels moved by a sacred force that the intellect does not recognize. This leaves the mystic radically divided, for he has a mysticism of love that excludes knowledge. A divided mystic can not be totally absorbed into God. But should the intellect know God, the will could do no other than love him. "If we know God and do not love him, what we know is not God" (AT, 281). This union of knowing and love would enable the mystic to be united within one's self and thus absorbed

remains formally an act of the intellect" (AT, 191). "Although contemplation consists, of course, in an act of the intelligence, not of the will, it is nevertheless true to say that in practice the most important element in the contemplative is not knowledge but love" (AT, 274).

into God. This union that includes both knowledge and love is the goal of the mystic (AT, 274, 281, 314).

When the will is being carried by God, one tends to think this is perfect contemplation. But it is not; it is only the Prayer of Quiet (what *Seeds of Contemplation* called *quietud sabrosa* [SC, 181]). The Prayer of Quiet is the beginning of mysticism, the borderland of mysticism, but not complete mysticism. In some sense this prayer can be called mysticism, for God is acting directly in the will. (Mysticism always involves the direct action of God, so that "natural mysticism" is a contradiction in terms [HGL, 470]). God is directly moving the will and not the intellect. The will is saying, "I know him," while the intellect is still searching. Yet, since one is divided, this is not the final form of contemplation. It is not a complete absorption into God, for the intellect has been excluded. The aim of the mystic is "the right ordering of man's whole being," and this can only happen when reason (the highest faculty) has subjected every other faculty to itself and then is absorbed in God. Only then can one love God with one's whole mind and heart and strength (AT, 156). Anti-rational forms of mysticism make this impossible by "fencing off one section of (one's) being as a sanctuary and leaving the rest to its own devices" (AT, 112). It is the whole person, body and soul, that must belong to God.

Reason, as the highest faculty, must supervise the ordering of the entire human being. So Merton often speaks of reason as the key to the mystical life (AT, 161, 181). It is the key for it alone can regulate the use of creatures and thus guide the other faculties. The intellect recognizes the goal of complete absorption into God, that is, a loving of God with the whole mind, heart and spirit. In infused contemplation God alone is acting, but the intellect has brought the mystic to this place. Merton would compare the mystic to a musical instrument that is played by the Holy Spirit. The Spirit of God makes all of the music, but reason has tuned the strings. "The Master Himself does not waste time tuning the instrument" (AT, 182). The mind has had to use its independence to critically evaluate what is going on, and finally to surrender, a surrender that is again an act of the intellect.

In contemplation God is acting in the intellect. But that does not mean that reasoning, argumentation and new insights are involved. The fulfillment of reason is found when it embraces the truth simply and without labor in the light of a single intuition. This is what occurs in contemplation, so one definition of contemplation would be a *simplex intuitus veritatis,* a simple intuition of the truth (AT, 205; MZM, 203).

The intellect must act according to the truth it sees, and yet it must go further. This it does by faith, an act of the understanding that takes one beyond what one understands. So Merton would claim that faith is between knowing and not knowing. It is the paradoxical unity wherein the human reaches beyond oneself and into God. By faith one moves towards that complete knowing wherein we shall "know God even as we are known." Then there will be no more darkness and no more paradox.

When God moves the intellect, the whole human being, body and soul, falls into place. This Merton found in St. Thomas (NM, 50). In the lower forms of mysticism our will (or our intellect and will) are passive and find it difficult to act (AT, 230). While in the final form of infused contemplation, our intellect and will are completely unable to act on their own. Merton would speak of them as "crippled." But considerable subtlety is needed in arriving at this passivity of infused contemplation. Quietists would disagree and urge that from the beginning the intellect should rest in the passivity of an unknowing. But Merton believed that one should not be passive unless there was reason to believe God would act in the faculty. Yet all of this activity should be ordered to the moment when the intelligence is passive and God is active. But again there is paradox: one is both active and passive; one is doing nothing and doing everything, (see AT, 223); one is oneself and Another.

Shortly after bringing out *The Ascent to Truth,* Merton brought out a book on the Psalms, *Bread in the Wilderness.* This considered again the issues of contemplation and the intellect. Prayer was said to be more than a union of wills with God, for "prayer demands intelligence." Only when intelligence is involved is our *whole* nature and its faculties fulfilled (BW, 13). Accordingly, in praying the Psalms, we must look to their *theological* rather than their psychological impact. And again contemplation is said to be founded upon dogmatic truth (BW, 28,

41). *Bread in the Wilderness* speaks abundantly of love for God, but this love is dependent on the intellect: it "flows from a knowledge of God as he is in himself" (BW, 107).

As in *The Ascent, Bread in the Wilderness* tells of the will being united with God before the intellect. This was the incomplete mysticism termed the Prayer of Quiet in *The Ascent,* but in *Bread in the Wilderness* it is termed "living faith." Merton used the gospel account of the Easter appearance of Jesus to his disciples on the road to Emmaus to tell of two different levels of prayer. At first the disciples felt "their eyes were held and they did not know him," but nevertheless "their heart was burning within them." This would seem to be the Prayer of Quiet. Only later "their eyes were opened and they knew him." This suggests the involvement of the intellect. Merton would see the first recognition as that of living faith and the second as "a good analogy for mystical contemplation properly so called" (BW, 117). In the experience of living faith "our eyes are held"; that is, our intellect is not fulfilled, though our hearts (wills) burn within us.

While the soul is in living faith, the burning love is a sign that God is near. So the soul seeks God intently "with a more or less enlightened ardor"; it looks into the texts of Scripture and the prayers of the liturgy to be further enlightened. One lives habitually in a state of burning ardor, but still one knows only a "veiled" contemplation that is not consciously aware of its own possibilities. But the ardor enables the mind to discover new riches in the Scriptures. And if we respond to our spiritual impulses, we find "they lovingly retain and hold us, for long thoughtless moments." Our minds are being enlightened. Our hearts are being absorbed in a simple gaze upon God whose love holds us captive by an unworldly charm. While so held there are sudden illuminations that Merton terms flashes of dark lightning, momentary recognitions. And then in one second of eternity "the whole soul is illumined by the tremendous darkness which is the light of God." Then we experience the full truth that hitherto we had only believed. This is a moment of infused contemplation; when the intellect is enlightened "the whole soul is transfixed and illumined" (BW, 119).

There are an abundance of texts that speak of our union with God being centered on both the intellect and will: e.g.: in 1954 union with God was located in "the apex of man's inmost intellect and will . . . that insatiable little diamond of spiritual awareness which is the most precious thing in the spirit of man" (NM, 120). Merton began to stress the importance of studies claiming that in monasteries "where theological study is neglected, contemplation is also at a rather low ebb." It was a fatal mistake to suppose that "a monk can discard books altogether and let his mind lie fallow all his life." The contemplative should be formed by "a deep intellectual appreciation of dogma and the understanding of theology" (CS, 1985, xx, 219). He even warned against setting up an arbitrary division between one's intellectual life and one's life of prayer (SCh, 177).

In 1958 Merton wrote to Pope John XXIII proposing the pope set up an apostolic foundation of contemplative monks who would invite writers and other intellectuals for conferences and discussion in the cloister. But he urged this monastery would have to be "in an Order that is strictly contemplative" (HGL, 483). The proposal makes sense only in the belief that contemplation had an intelligible content; so presumably these contemplatives would be familiar with the metaphysical intuition considered in the previous section, for it alone gives one a content.

In 1961 Merton brought out a substantial revision of *Seeds of Contemplation* entitled *New Seeds of Contemplation.* The opening sentence of *New Seeds* affirms, "Contemplation is the highest expression of man's *intellectual* and spiritual life" (emphasis added). Contemplation is said to *know* the transcendent Source of all things. "Both reason and faith aspire, by their very nature" to contemplation and would be incomplete without it. Yet contemplation is again paradoxical, for it "knows without knowing." The speech of the contemplative "takes back what it has said, and denies what it has affirmed" (NSC, 1). For contemplation is a *knowing* beyond knowing and unknowing (NSC, 2).

In the original text (old *Seeds*—as quoted above), Merton had claimed "nothing that we can know" with our natural faculties can be other than an obstacle to contemplation; this claim is deleted from the revised text (compare SC, 123; NSC, 209). Old *Seeds* had told of unlearned Trappists often being better contemplatives than those with much learning. *New*

Seeds states this claim—and then dismisses it as a familiar cliche. In *New Seeds*—and not in old *Seeds*—we are told, "learning has an important part to play in the contemplative life" (compare SC, 160; NSC, 253). A new passage has been added that develops the point:

> Contemplation, far from being opposed to theology, is in fact the normal perfection of theology. We must not separate intellectual study of divinely revealed truth and contemplative experience of that truth as if they could never have anything to do with one another. On the contrary they are simply two aspects of the same thing (NSC, 254).

It must be acknowledged that the earlier *Seeds* had told of the importance of the intellect in contemplation (see SC, 72). But the changes Merton made in his own text show better than anything else his increasing awareness of this importance. He was coming to accept the intellectual life that once had set him apart from his fellow Trappists. He would speak from experience when telling of "the fearsome difficulties of intellectuals in the cloister" (CS; 1987, xxii, 68). Yet he would insist that the monks develop their intellects. A final book on contemplation would claim, "The spiritual life needs strong intellectual foundations" (CP, 79).

Merton found the word "truth" present throughout the monastic tradition and told of it resounding "in the profoundest depths of the monastic heart" (SL, 21). It is clearly an intellectual word, and it echoes through the texts of Merton (see for example CGB, 68, 69, 78, 80, 84, 85, 91, 93, 111, 117, etc. and especially 184; see SL, 21–25). Monks were identified as those who saw around them a world of "collective unreason" and left this world to seek "truth for its own sake." But they were not seeking an abstract truth; they sought the truth that would absorb all of one's faculties. The contemplative could be identified as "the one who seeks to know the meaning of life not only with his head but with his whole being" (R, 401). Such is the *knowing* of the contemplative.

During his twenty some years as a writer, Merton moved further and further from the scholastic tradition that once was central to his thought. He would eventually express a reluctance to direct anyone purely along the lines of St. John of the

Cross (HGL, 351). But like the scholastics and John of the Cross, he continued to speak of the importance of both knowing and the intellect. Those who regarded the mind as an obstacle to contemplation were said to be making "a big mistake" that would lead to unfortunate results (HGL, 361). And the mistake is that if the mind is not involved, one would be divided against oneself. Contemplation must eventually be the act of one's whole being, and the intellect (or the intellect and the will) is the faculty of this union.

In the final years of Merton's life, some Christian writers known as "God is dead" theologians appealed to the apophatic tradition in Christian theology to justify their claim. But Merton was not impressed. He acknowledged some parallel with the apophatic tradition, but would not allow the tradition of unknowing stand by itself.

> . . . this tradition of mystical negation always coexists, in Christianity, with a tradition of symbolic theology in which positive symbols and analogies of theological teaching are accepted for what they are: true but imperfect approximations which lead us gradually towards that which cannot be expressed in human language (FV, 269).

The role of the intellect came up again two months before he died; in a conference Merton told of looking for "the final integration and unification of man in love." And for this integration he claimed one must "develop a heart that knows God, not just a heart that loves God, but a heart that knows God" (TMA, 147, 153).

This knowing might be far more experiential than the knowing found in the earlier Merton; it might be far less involved in the faculty psychology of scholasticism; it might avoid terms like natural and supernatural; it might be far more open to traditions with radically different teachings, but Merton continued to say that beyond the knowing and the unknowing of the contemplative—*there is a knowing.*

Contemplation in Art and Life

Merton would compare the soul in contemplation to Adam and Eve in Paradise (NSC, 229; NM, 37; CS, 1983, xviii, 201;

Intro to CG, xii). Adam and Eve recognized the value of everything, for like God they saw everything to be good. Merton waxed eloquent in telling of Paradise:

> Dolphins played in the waters. Rare birds flew up out of the marshes. . . . Wild horses ran in their herds like wind upon the prairies. The glades gave up their deer as the leopard came down to the stream to quench her thirst (NM, 37).

Adam was placed in Paradise to live and breathe in unison with God. He saw that God was all and that nothing else mattered. So everything was seen to be beautiful and good. Adam had a perfect knowledge of the world and his will acted in perfect conformity with his vision. By Adam's knowing them, all things in the surrounding world were raised to the level of intelligibility and value. Thus, Adam was the priest offering it all to God. And he met God continually "in flashes of mystical intuition either in the existential reality of his own spiritual depths or in the reality of objective creation." His knowledge of God was twofold: he knew the transcendence of God in his eternal Word and the immanence of God in all creatures. Thus he had both supernatural and natural contemplation. He did not find his times of infused awareness to be a violent interruption of his routine: "in Paradise ecstasy is normal" (NM, 39).

Merton would frequently speak of contemplation as a return to Paradise; in this he followed Cassian and many other Church Fathers. Those who return to Paradise would find "the lost innocence, the emptiness and the purity of heart" which had belonged to Adam and Eve in Eden (R, 481–482). They would still live on earth, but, because they had regained their innocence, their natural vision would be free from deception and all things would be seen in God. But there would be times when they would be raised to infused contemplation and know God as he is in himself.

Since contemplation is essentially a free act, Adam had to consent to the divine illumination. This divine illumination continued as long as he permitted no lie to come between God and himself. But Paradise did not last. Adam wilfully accepted unreality; his fall was his consent "to receive and even prefer a lie to the truth" (NM, 50). Merton would regularly speak of the lie as the root of all sin; this too shows the centrality of the intellect. Adam had known only the good, but, by eating of the tree of knowledge of good and evil, he came to know both. Thus by his sin Adam and his descendants came to live in an ambiguous world, a world seen as both true and false. For Merton sin is fundamentally a preference for the false: "every sin is a sin against truth" (NMI, 84). The early desert monks went to live in the wilderness, not to avoid the world, but to avoid the warped understanding that governs the human city.

Creation was originally given to humans "as a clean window through which the light of God" could shine. "Sun and moon, night and day, rain, the sea, the crops, the flowering tree, all these things were transparent" (BW, 60). All nature was a symbol. But with the fall of Adam the world also fell: nature became opaque. People were no longer able to penetrate the deep meaning of the world in which they lived. Instead of seeing the sun and moon as witnesses of the power of God, they thought the sun and moon themselves were gods. Nature was divinized. Soon the whole universe became a system of enclosed myths that no longer spoke of anything beyond Nature. Darkness settled upon the transcendent universe. The world still seemed to be full of meanings that no one could understand, so people began devising superstitious rites. They developed magic incantations to placate and control the mysterious powers of nature.

Thus the window to heaven became darkened. The universe was not seen for what it was; humans were lost in a labyrinth of myths and magic ceremonies. The world no longer spoke of God but only of human doings.

> The *symbols* which would have raised man above himself to God now became *myths* and as such they were simply projections of man's own biological drives. His deepest appetites, now full of shame, became his darkest fears (BW, 61).

Merton compares the change to what happens when a room ceases to receive light from the outside. As long as it was day, those inside could see through the windowpane. When night comes they can see through it only if there is no light inside the room. But when the light in the room is on, they see only the reflection of themselves and the room. People began to forget the sky and they lighted lamps of their own. Soon they took their reflections in the window to be the real world: "they began to worship what they themselves were doing."

Though the world had become opaque, Merton would see some of the original purity remaining in the great religions of the East, but to maintain that purity they had to dismiss the world as illusion. Buddha recognized that the reflections in the window were only projections of our own desires, so he was ruthless in dismissing these. But he did not know that the world was meant to be a window and that sunlight can be seen beyond the glass.

Merton believed the Psalms presented the cosmic symbols shining clear and bright. There the heavens still proclaim the glory of God and the stars still testify to his handiwork. The psalms have a special ability to enable us to see things as they are and thus lead us to contemplation. For brief moments they can show us the original Paradise where all things manifest God. But then we return to seeing the familiar world as a collection of things to be loved for their own sake. For we have been blinded by our myths and a great purification is needed so that once again we may look on the world with "purity of heart." The Gospel says, "Blessed are the pure of heart, for they shall see God." This was an important text for both Merton and the desert Fathers; they would seek purity of heart, for this would enable them to return to Paradise and see God and the world as Adam and Eve had seen them.

Merton judged most of what is known as the modern world to be a farrago of deceit and illusion—again, sin begins in the intellect. Fictitious events are created by journalists, and slogans are devised by advertisers. "We are surrounded with fake objects which we continue, out of sheer boredom and inertia, to 'inspect,' to 'study,' to 'evaluate,' thus perpetuating the mystification" (CGB, 256). We are so surrounded by illusions that in seeking the truth we do not know how to begin. "The city" is a conspiracy of deceit, a place that devises the mythology of power and war. There tired, frustrated, and angry people are caught in the movement of hot traffic surrounding a place "where anger and bewilderment are concentrated in a neon lit air-conditioned enclave, glittering with 'products,' humming with piped-in music, and reeking of the nondescript, sterile, and sweet smell of the technologically functioning world" (CGB, 257, 138). City people are slaves to this illusion, careful to think only the right thoughts and wear the right hat: it is a "crude and shameful concern not with truth but only with vogue" (CGB, 284). This is "the world" we have made for ourselves: appearance is everything and appearance must be all encompassing to maintain our illusion. The whole structure of modern life is aimed at leaving us alienated from ourselves and God. It is "a complete and systematic sham" (NMI, 109; CGB, 339). "The city itself lives on its own myth." Its people live the fabricated dream they maintain only by sharing it with each other. "They have constructed a world outside the world, against the world, a world of mechanical fictions which contemn nature"[13] (RU, 11).

Merton believed there was a deep truth beneath the dehumanized surface of things. But the deep relationship of all things to God is being stifled by systematic illusion. In speaking of the "world" or the "city," Merton allowed there was more to each than what he considered, but he wanted to focus "on the sham, the unreality, the alienation, the forced systematization of life." He saw people so preoccupied with this surface agitation that they could not recognize their own estrangement from the deep goodness that remains in Nature and themselves (CGB, 257). Nature still proclaims its ongoing goodness, and this goodness is to be found as the deeper identity of each thing: "The special clumsy beauty of this particular colt on this April day in this field under these clouds . . . declares the glory of God" (NSC, 30). But individual things are not seen for themselves at all, because we are each preoccupied with dreams of power and live by slogans, illusions, and fashions. We need a purity of heart to see through this artificial world.

If we develop an interior life, we begin to recognize the truth and value in ordinary things; then their beauty becomes simple and obvious. But to sustain this beauty we must unlearn

---

[13]Merton read Jacques Ellul's study *La Technique* and found Ellul too pessimistic. He added that technology is not unholy; it is simply neutral (VC, 93–99). He seemed a little surprised when someone criticized his negative references to technology (RJ, 98).

false ways of seeing, tasting and feeling: "we first have to learn to see life as if it were something more than a hypnotizing telecast" (NMI, 33). Contemplation is a direct experience of reality at its ultimate root, so contemplation is necessary if people are to remain human. Order, peace, sanity, and happiness follow from the contemplation by which one gains a spiritual orientation in life. "But true contemplation is an austere and exacting vocation. Those who seek it are few and those who find it are fewer still" (HR, 85). The contemplative must break free of the common spell of the city and see a value that makes one stand apart: "to be a contemplative therefore is to be an outlaw. As was Christ. As was [St.] Paul" (RU, 14).

In telling of the need for detachment, Merton followed a common monastic tradition. The early Christian monks went to the wilderness for they judged city culture to be "a shipwreck from which each single individual man had to swim for his life" (WD, 3). They refused the passive acceptance of what the cities proclaimed and went to the desert "to be themselves, their *ordinary* selves, and to forget a world that divided themselves against themselves" (WD, 23). They sought purity of heart and recited the psalms, and gradually the simplicity of their lives and the clean images of the psalter helped restore their ability to see the true meaning of things.

Merton found the modern world to be radically opposed to the monastic ideal. He believed advertisers were consciously trying to blind our intellect and destroy our ability to recognize moral values. They bombard our senses with artificial stimulation that keep our nerves at a dazzling level of intensity. Perhaps we recognize we are being pushed into an excess of consumerism and develop a "protective insensibility" just to survive. Merton saw the whole of American culture opposed to contemplation, for it conceals the deeper truth. But it is not just a matter of avoiding things that are sinful and ordering our life according to reason. "A man who hopes to become a contemplative by detaching himself only from the things that are forbidden by reason will not even begin to know the meaning of contemplation" (NSC, 208). Reason might restore us to a natural level of contemplation, but to recover the innocence of Adam in Paradise, one must cross an abyss of ascetic detachment (NSC, 209).

Ascetic detachment implies a discipline. So Merton would tell of the contemplative life requiring "a special dimension of inner discipline," "some real contemplative discipline" (CWA, 172; RJ, 109). Without discipline "no serious meditation will be possible" (SDM, iii). Mental prayer requires "constant and strict interior discipline," and this means a mortification of the senses (SDM, 68, 70). Monastic life included an obligation to discipline (MJ, 44). Merton found similar demands being made by the sages of Asia: the Dalai Lama told him of the need for "real discipline," and a Cambodian Buddhist told him of the importance of "disciplining the mind" (RJ, 119, 120). Adam did not need to discipline his mind, but today anyone serious about contemplation must learn an interior discipline.

Poetry, music and art can enable us to come to natural contemplation. The art object appears in the midst of ordinary life and there reveals a transcendent meaning. A symbol is seen in the midst of things, but it takes us beyond things. Art and poetry introduce one to the deeper truth of the world. They can attune one to God, for they reveal the living law that rules the universe.

> This law is nothing but the secret gravitation that draws all things to God as to their center. Since all true art lays bare the action of this same law in the depths of our own nature, it makes us alive to the tremendous mystery of being, in which we ourselves, together with all other living and existing things, come forth from the depths of God and return again to Him. An art which does not produce something of this is not worthy of its name (NMI, 36).

Merton believed the artist should reveal this deeper truth. In this he was again following Maritain and trying to understand his own writing poetry. Merton did not see the artist and poet as creators of illusion; they were only revealing the truth that we no longer recognize. Merton believed we all have an innate capacity to sense God present in the world. But this "inmost need and capacity for contemplation" is what we can lose by modern life (HR, 89). This capacity "needs to be brought to life by the proper signs and symbols" (NM, 56). The words of the poet can serve as "seeds of prayer and contemplation." For the primary function of the word is contemplative, rather than communicative; and the primary function of language is to witness to the hidden meaning of things. Speech should be "a kind of seal upon our intellectual communion" with God. Our whole sense of the "numinous" depends on our own ability to read signs and symbols and transcend them to "pass beyond their manifest intelligibility into the darkness of mystery, to grasp the reality they can suggest but never fully contain" (NM, 57).

But the city has no time for contemplation, mystery and the deeper identity of things. In the world of illusion the poet is the outlaw. He writes apart from the "officially subsidized culture" (CGB, 283). He sees beyond the popular slogans and illusions; he speaks from an ingrained innocence and tells the culture what it does not want to see. The poet has nothing to do with the "magic of words." All such conjuring is for the propagandist. The true poet will enable us to see beyond the social magic that holds us enthralled (RU, 159).

The aesthetic experience takes one beyond the sensible order to reveal things in their perfection, and this is a form of contemplation. The aesthetic experience is also "an analogue of the mystical experience which it resembles and imitates from afar" (R, 407). It too reaches out to grasp the inner reality of its object by a kind of identification of itself with the object. This can resemble the "immediate affective contact with God in the obscurity of mystical prayer." Merton believed the poetic and religious contacts are so similar that a poet like William Blake could confuse the two.

The poet or the artist penetrates to the reality of things, and Merton allowed they might be able to reach God himself. He found this in conformity with what the Greek Fathers wrote in telling of a "natural contemplation" that arrives at God through the inner reality (the *logos*) of the created thing. Things are again seen as symbols. His point is that one can pass from objective knowledge to "knowledge by intuition and connaturality" (R, 409). This resembles the knowledge found in infused contemplation. The aesthetic experience introduces us into the inner sanctuary of our own soul, and from there we can pass to God. So Merton would claim that "art enables us to find and lose ourselves at the same time" (NMI, 34). In seeing a symbol, we see it, and then see beyond it. When we see our-

selves as symbol or as image of God, we immediately pass beyond to the God we image. True art leads us to the inner sanctuary of what it reveals to us. "For the aesthetic intuition is
also beyond objectivity—it 'sees' by identifying itself spiritually with what it contemplates" (R, 409; NMI, 34). Thus the
natural contemplation of the artist gives one a taste of the in-
toxication of contemplation; it prepares the way for infused
contemplation. Both art and contemplation involve an "identification with," and this identification is apart from the division between subject and object.

Merton even told of the need to develop one's imagination;
it was necessary for the Christian life or any life (SCh, 231).
This is in contrast to the apophatic tradition that he generally
followed (e.g.: *The Cloud of Unknowing:* "suppress the imagination"). Significant literature, music, and art can help the
contemplative develop (CWA, 358). These should be part of
the contemplative; so "casting prudence to the wind" Merton
lectured the novices on art and his fellow monks on the poems
of Rilke and Eliot (C&L, tape; SCh, 231). Poetry can purify
the heart and restore our childlike vision of innocence.

Merton developed the similarities between the aesthetic experience and contemplation in reflecting on a poem by Rilke.
Rilke wrote of an "out gazing" that is proper to the child. But
Rilke saw culture teaching the child "to 'be opposite,' to *stand
against* objects and never be anything but a subject confront-
ing objects" (MZM, 244). This "spectatorship" with its attendant "self-consciousness"—our Cartesian heritage—is a
wound in our nature, a "kind of original sin" for which "healing" is urgently required. But if our identity as a self-conscious
spectator is the only identity we can recognize, we will refuse
all healing lest we cease to exist. For since the Fall, the human
has seen himself "as a kind of pseudo object from which he was
estranged" (CS, 1983, xviii, 201). But apart from this identity
there is a "pure consciousness" that does not look at self or
things; it identifies with them. Then "the subject is aware of itself as having penetrated by poetic empathy into the heart of
the object and being united with it" (MZM, 245). One rests at
the center of what is contemplated "where God is sitting and
saying it is good" (C&L, tape).

The poet's ability to enter the identity of the other has evident parallels with the infused contemplation considered earlier in this chapter. There an extended analogy was drawn between contemplation and the listening by which one identifies with a speaker. Here the poet is one who is able to identify with the inner truth of things; he shares this identity with his readers. It follows that the poet or the artist will be better prepared than most to receive infused contemplation—should God grant it. And even the artist's refined sensibility can help one avoid the common mistakes of other mystics.

But there are also difficulties for the artist. In tasting infused contemplation the instincts of the artist are no longer a help. The mystic enters contemplation to lose one's self in the transcendent God, while the artist enters *to work,* to act, to create. If one is both mystic and artist, one would be inclined to withdraw from union and return to the world of human activity and objectify what one has found. In the process one has left contemplation. The instincts of the artist have opposed the passing beyond self into infused contemplation. Merton explains by appeal to the fable of the hare and the tortoise. At first the artist can outstrip the non artist, but in the end there is danger that the artist might stop before coming to full contemplation (R, 412). At first Art might deliver the artist from the banalities of ordinary culture. But soon one's involvement with images interferes with the ability to rest in the God "beyond all images."

In contemplation one simply listens (or gazes)—while the artist both listens and speaks (or gazes and paints). Yet Merton came to accept his active work as a writer as his particular vocation—yet allowed that others were called to a better way (see above). But in 1964 he went further when he wrote to the theologian von Balthasar asking if this speaking (painting) was not essential to the process: "Theoria [contemplation] demands not just gazing but response and statement. Don't you agree?" (SCh, 219). Contemplation is still listening (gazing), but now the listening demands a response; contemplation has become one part of a dialogue! (At times this dialogue is called meditation. See CP, 38 and *Enchantments,* 154–160.)

After writing abundantly of contemplation, Merton feared that he had contributed to the general mystification whereby contemplation became an objective thing that might get "interfered with." He feared lest he had set up the myth of "contemplation with a capital C," a "thing" apart from the rest of life, a safe and somewhat bourgeois cause to which one might dedicate oneself! (R, 401).

> In actual fact, true contemplation is inseparable from life and from the dynamism of life—which includes work, creation, production, fruitfulness, and above all *love*. Contemplation is not to be thought of as a separate department of life, cut off from all man's other interests and superseding them. It is the very fullness of a fully integrated life. It is the crown of life and of all life's activities (R, 400).

The early monks made a radical break with their cultures and went apart for a healing of their vision. Merton made a similar break in entering the monastery. His early works insist on the importance of a break with the world in order to contemplate; his later works would introduce contemplation back into ordinary life. As Merton's thought developed, contemplation became less a way of leaving the world than the only sane way of living in it. Beyond contemplation taking him out of the world, he believed contemplation had something to say to the world. He accepted himself as a creative writer; and hoped his art would reveal the deeper meaning in things.

Though contemplation might be discovered within the monastic enclosure, it was not to remain there: "the contemplative life applies wherever there is life" (HR, 39). For all humans are striving to find significance in life. And for our deeds and concerns to be significant . . .

> the independent significance of each must converge in some way into a central and universal significance which comes from a hidden reality. This central reality has to be a 'catholic' reality, a 'divine' reality. The reality central to my life is the life of God. To know this is the contemplative's objective (HR, 39).

Merton knew that his own vocation was unusual, but he believed he had a message for everyone. He objected to mystical writings that were completely out of touch with ordinary life. For "mysticism flourishes most purely right in the middle of the ordinary" (HGL, 621). He faulted his earlier books: "precisely what was lacking was the Zen element" (SCh, 167).

Contemplation is not a commodity for the chosen few, but the goal of all who try to find significance in spite of themselves in the Living God. It does not make sense to the world, for it does not accomplish the goals that the world has set for itself. But the contemplative and the poet can remind the world of the Ultimate that is simply there. This is what our nation needs to recognize. For "without contemplation, without the intimate, silent, secret pursuit of truth through love," the American nation will become inhuman. While contemplation can reveal to us what Adam saw in Paradise. Then we can come together as we were meant to be. "In Adam all men were to be, as it were, 'one contemplative,' perfectly united to one another in their one vision and love of one truth" (Intro, CG, xii).

Cont. is a goal for those who for significance in God

3

Freedom

The free man does not float
On the tides of his own expedition
Nor is he sent on adventures as busy men are,
Bound to an inexorable result.

Merton opened his autobiography by giving the date and place of his birth; then he stated the theme of the book: "Free by nature, in the image of God, I was nevertheless the prisoner of my own violence and my own selfishness in the image of the world into which I was born." Thus Merton knew himself as both image of God and image of the world. His autobiography would tell of passing from one image to the other; it was the story of a prisoner gaining his freedom.

The Prisoner of Selfishness

Merton's mother died when Tom was six years old, and in the years that followed he and his younger brother led an unsettled life. Their father was a struggling artist who sometimes took Tom with him on painting trips to New England, Bermuda, or Europe; sometimes he left Tom with his grandparents in Douglaston, Long Island, and sometimes he put him in a boarding school in France or England. Tom was always serious about studies, but otherwise he had little discipline. He read the novels of Hemingway, Joyce and, D. H. Lawrence, and from these developed what he termed his "philosophy of pleasure."

In 1932, upon graduating from Oakham, an English boarding school, and before beginning studies at Cambridge, the young Merton set out on a free-wheeling trip across Europe. He wanted to test his new philosophy. But after a month of trying to enjoy himself, he became disgusted by the "precious liberty" he set out to enjoy. In Rome he visited the Church of St. Peter in Chains and felt bound by heavier chains.

> So there I was with all the liberty that I had been promising myself for so long. The world was mine. How did I like it? I was doing just what I pleased, and instead of being filled with happiness and well-being, I was miserable (SSM, 106).

He soon became fascinated by the austere Byzantine mosaics of Rome and was haunting the churches where they were found. He was living in a small *pensione* and reading the Gospels. One night he had a strange sense that his dead father was present in his room. This brought him to a recognition of the misery and corruption within his soul. His wanton living seemed free of restraints, yet his "soul desired escape and liberation and freedom." He began to pray when he visited the churches. But he felt imprisoned by "the thousand terrible things that held (his) will in their slavery" (SSM, 111).

Returning to England and university studies, Merton soon resumed his dissipation: "I was trying with all of my might to crush and obliterate the image of the divine liberty that had been planted in me by God" (SSM, 121). At Cambridge he got himself into serious trouble that he does not explain. It seems he fathered a child, but biographers have been unable to identify the trouble with complete success. Merton has told of lawyers reaching a settlement, and his English guardian urged him to continue his studies in the United States. So Merton moved to his grandparents' home in Long Island and enrolled at Columbia University. There he liked the professors, the courses, and many fellow students; it was a happy time for Merton the scholar. Yet his behavior was compulsive: he tells of movie posters enticing him into seeing most of the movies produced between 1934 and 1937. But he would hardly be in the theater until he was appalled by the "colossal stupidities" on the screen. Yet the following day he would return to the movies. He compared it to a smoker lighting a cigarette and being disgusted by the taste; one puts the cigarette out—and lights another (see NSC, 85, 86). He started suffering from real and imaginary diseases and became hyper-conscious of his diet. Finally, a romantic rejection made him look at his life:

> I had at last become a true child of the modern world, completely tangled up in petty and useless concerns with myself, and almost incapable of even considering or understanding anything that was really important to my true interests.
> Here I was, scarcely four years after I had left Oakham and walked out into the world that I thought I was going to ransack and rob of all its pleasures and satisfactions. I had done what I had intended, and now I found that it was I who was emptied and robbed and gutted (SSM, 163–64).

During his early years at Columbia Merton had considered himself an atheist, but he soon developed an academing interest in medieval philosophy and literature and these would lead him to Catholicism. He read a book by Aldous Huxley on mysticism, *Ends and Means;* it proposed a philosophy of *freedom* that eventually would become his own. Merton had liked Huxley's novels and knew of the agnostic background of the Huxley family (his grandfather invented the term), so he was surprised that Huxley would be sympathetic with the mystics. Huxley said we must "fight our way free" from subjection to our animal appetites: only by self control can the soul gain its "freedom of action." He called for asceticism and discipline, but not as ends in themselves. They were

> . . . a freeing, a vindication of our real selves, a liberation of the spirit from limits and bonds that were intolerable, suicidal—from a servitude to flesh that must ultimately destroy our whole nature and society and the world as well (Merton's recollection of Huxley; SSM, 186).

Merton knew he needed "liberation" and began speaking enthusiastically to his friends about mysticism, but all the while he felt "completely chained and fettered" by sins and attachments (SSM, 205).

Merton decided to begin instructions in Catholicism and saw his baptism as a "liberation" from the slavery to death. In a vague way he started considering the priesthood. He read about different religious orders and concluded that what he needed was a religious rule aimed at detaching him from the world that restrained his freedom. He was fascinated (and terrified) when he first heard of the Trappists. After a visit to the monastery in April 1941, he applied for admission in November. Europe was at war and, though Merton's health was poor, he knew he might be drafted. The monastery invited him to come for a period of trial, but as he made preparations to leave upstate New York, the Japanese bombed Pearl Harbor and the United States was engulfed in World War II. Events were out of his hands; yet he was free of events. During the long train ride from New York to Kentucky, he felt an intense desire for monastic life:

> And for all the tremendous and increasing intensity of my desire to be in the cloister, the thought that I might find myself, instead, in an army camp no longer troubled me in the least. I was free. I had recovered my liberty. I belonged to God, not to myself: and to belong to Him is to be free, free of all the anxieties and worries and sorrows that belong to this earth, and the love of things that are in it. . . . The only thing that mattered was the fact of the sacrifice, the essential dedication of one's self, one's will. The rest was only accidental (SSM, 370).

His dedication was his liberation. Events might overtake him—but by his commitment to God his spirit was free. He felt free of attachments as he arrived at the monastery in the late evening of December 10. "Freedom to move around was not the freedom I was looking for" (MAG, 213). The porter received him at the door and the gate was locked behind him: "I was enclosed in the four walls of my freedom." He walked across a monastery yard that was dark and cold, but it was an appropriate beginning for his new life: "I entered a garden that was dead and stripped and bare."

Merton's philosophy of pleasure left him in bondage to the things of earth. He was victimized by advertisers who produced tantalizing images that kept him continually discontented and reaching for more. He was free not to buy, but he hardly recognized this freedom as he responded to each allurement. His behavior had become automatic, yet he was seeking freedom. "When I give myself what I conceive to be freedom, I deceive myself and find that I am the prisoner of my own blindness and selfishness and insufficiency" (NMI, 24). His pleasures left him empty and disgusted with himself; yet he felt unable to change. His wanton life had made him a slave.

> The slave, in the spiritual order, is the man whose choices have destroyed all spontaneity in him and have delivered him over, bound hand and foot, to his own compulsions, idiosyncracies and illusions, so that he never does what he really wants to do, but only what he has to do. His spirit is not in command, and therefore he cannot run his own life. He is commanded by his own weak flesh and its passions—fear, greed, lust, insecurity, untruthfulness, envy, cruelty, servility, and all the rest (NM, 105).

He was responding blindly to every stimulation that was offered. He was in bondage to his lusts, angers and hatreds. But by the grace of God he found deliverance. And Merton would insist that it was a grace; it was not deserved. It was a gift of God's mercy—not of his justice. Mercy is free; it is God acting freely to set us free from our obsessions. Divine mercy breaks into "the obsessive world which we have 'made up' for ourselves by yielding to our obsessions" (RU, 32). By knowing God as Mercy one discovers the freedom of God, and thereby one becomes free. Our freedom is a participation in the freedom of God (SC, 110).

But still we need a personal discipline. (This was treated in the previous section.) And unless the discipline is severe, "it will never set us free from the passions" (NM, 112). A discipline enables us to master our impulses. Merton had no sympathy with the "situation ethics" that would urge us to be open to the feeling of the moment. For Merton this was only an infantile regression that left us bound to our appetites. He had no sympathy with those monks who wanted monastic life without asceticism: "throwing away all of these practices and living in a kind of freedom of spirit without any real discipline is fatal." In contrast he would tell of the early desert monks who had "become free by paying the price" (WD, 11). Monks today must do the same. In short, "the freedom we look for is bound up with restrictions" (CWA, 372). The prescribed forms of the liturgy and even religious obedience were seen as ways to set the monk free (MJ, 85, 89, 94). We must be "ruthless in our determination to break all spiritual chains and cast off the domination of alien compulsions to find our true selves" (WD, 24). You practice asceticism in order "to do as you want" (CS, 1974, vol. ix., 56).

Our freedom is not to go off as a series of fireworks with no purpose or direction. Freedom is the ability to commit ourselves, to dedicate ourselves, "to surrender ourselves, to pay the supreme homage of our inmost being to what we have chosen as our good" (MJ, 77). To attain this the monk must set aside a superficial "freedom of choice" (e.g., freedom to travel) to discover a central "freedom of spontaneity" (a freedom to do what one really wills) (CS, 1974, vol. ix, 61). This is the freedom found only when one's freedom is in control.

When in bondage to the world, one is not able to make a decisive choice. For one is paralyzed when he or she tries to make a definitive act. Perhaps the passions dominate and act for one, and one's deeper self is unable to act. One's life is out of control; one is the victim of each new mood or desire. For "the flesh and the passions, of themselves, tend to anarchy, being at the mercy of sense stimulation." Such was Merton before his conversion, and to some extent after. In a general way Merton wanted to be a priest and talked on about the wonders of mysticism. Yet he was attached to the drinking, partying, and compulsive behavior that left him disgusted with himself. He wanted to live as a dedicated Catholic, but he felt incapable of changing. He wanted to be a priest, but he could take no step in the direction he wanted to go.

The Seven Storey Mountain tells of a day early in the fall of 1939 when Merton and some friends slept till noon after spending all night in a bar. As they ate their breakfast Merton announced he would become a priest. One friend had heard it before and thought he was fooling, and in a sense he was—for he could not mean it. Then, Merton walked the streets of lower Manhattan, dropped in on another friend and told her the same news. She was more or less indifferent. So he wandered along Eighth Avenue and turned up Sixteenth Street; he entered the Church of St. Francis Xavier as Benediction was being celebrated. He knelt in prayer.

> And then it suddenly became clear to me that my whole life
> was at a crisis. Far more than I could imagine or understand
> or conceive was hanging upon a word—a decision of
> mine. . . . If I had hesitated or refused at that moment—
> what would have become of me? (SSM, 255).

The moment was not his own doing:

> I knew that I had been called in here abruptly to answer a
> question that had been preparing, not in my mind, but in the
> infinite depth of an eternal Providence.

His whole life seemed suspended on the edge of an abyss and
he was faced with the question, "Do you really want to be a
priest? If you do, say so. . . ." It was a moment of interroga-
tion. He heard the congregation begin the final hymn as he
tried to collect his thoughts. He looked at the host in the mon-
strance and said, "Yes, I want to be a priest, with all my heart I
want it." It was the one thing he had been unable to say. Until
this moment his heart had been divided. But for a moment he
was whole and present to himself. In his freedom he prayed,
"Make me your priest." By his response he knew a union had
been sealed between the Power he addressed and himself. He
was finally free to do what he had wanted to do, and his freedom seemed to be a gift *from* God. The gift enabled him to
make himself a gift *to* God. Later he would write, "We are
made for an act that gathers up all the powers and capacities of
our being and offers them up simultaneously and forever to
God" (NMI, 140).

Merton's "powers and capacities" had been scattered, but
the act for which he was made came as he knelt for Benediction
at the Church of St. Francis Xavier. There would be a similar
moment in November 1941 when he decided to enter the
Trappists. Each of these moments involved the presence of
God. That is, in choosing his vocation there were two wills involved, God's and his own. And both of them were free. Our
vocation is "the interaction of two freedoms" (NMI, 132).

For many months Merton had been struggling with an ineffective desire for the priesthood—for he was caught in worldly
entanglements. Then suddenly God was present and the entanglements of the world meant nothing; he was free to make a

real decision. The entanglements might return, but in the clean austerity of a moment a free decision was made. When he entered the monastery on a cold December night, the austerity of the garden symbolized the austerity needed to be free.

To achieve detachment is a long and difficult process. One begins with the abnegation of the five exterior senses, but Merton would have it that this is scarcely the beginning. Even in using created things in a rational and temperate way, we still can be attached to them. So, Merton argued, we must pass beyond ordinary temperance and strive for complete emptiness in order to "enter into the perfect freedom of the Sons of God." Then one lives "in emptiness, in freedom" as if one no longer had a limited self. Yet even monks who have renounced the pleasures and ambitions of the world can develop subtle pleasures and ambitions. They become attached to the good things of the monastic world, to the small routines of monastic life or to "interior peace" or "recollection," and though these might be good things or things of small importance, the monks are bound. If they are bound by less than God, they are not free.

For Merton freedom is the fundamental aim of the monk. He claimed that St. Bernard (best known of the twelfth-century Cistercians) saw freedom as the object of monastic discipline (MJ, 77). Merton reflected on the early Cistercians who left the cities and the large monasteries to find a remote place: "they were looking for freedom: freedom from all the cares and burdens of worldly business and ambition" (WS, 291). The monastery then became "a school of freedom," the place "where man learns to bear the weight of his own freedom," not to "renounce his freedom" (MJ, 107). In working with the young monks Merton insisted that the real question is not "Am I happy?" but "Am I free?" (Pennington, TMBM, 15: CS, 1974, vol. ix, 57).

Huxley's study of mysticism spoke of our attachment to things corrupting society. So Merton would see human tyranny as "the external expression of each man's enslavement to his own desires" (TMDP, 141). Merton saw Americans living as slaves to their appetites. He urged those unable to enter a monastery to have as little to do with radios, newspapers, and noise as possible—they are all part of our bondage. His view of American culture was radically negative: "the culture of the white man is not worth the dirt in Harlem's gutters" (SSM, 346). The age itself was caught in contradiction: It was dreaming about freedom, but dominated by compulsion. "Though we fight wars over it (freedom), our civilization is strictly servile" (CGB, 308). We talk of decision, but events decide for us: "instead of being men of *decision* we are men of *velleity.*" We act on desires that are weak and erratic. These ironies "ought to alert us to the fact that while we talk our heads off about freedom we have in fact surrendered to un-freedom" (CGB, 331). Such is the bondage Merton continued to disown.

The opening passage of *The Seven Storey Mountain* spoke of freedom as the image of God in the human. Merton saw this as the teaching of the Church Fathers (the Fathers were not in agreement about what made us the image of God),[14] and he identified this teaching more specifically with St. Gregory of Nyssa and St. Bernard (DQ, x; NM, 44). This identification runs throughout his writings. Perhaps the best way of understanding the claim is to recall Merton's account of attending Benediction and saying with all his heart he wanted to be a priest. He had been wanting to say that, but could not. Then sensing the presence of God, he was able to commit himself. He would explain, "we are most truly free in the free encounter of our hearts with God in his word" (HGL, 159). God seemed to be speaking words of invitation and in response Merton was able to speak what he had been wanting to say.[15] Merton did not believe he deserved grace. It was freely given; it came from

---

[14]Many Church Fathers, picking up the phrase from Genesis 1:26, spoke of our souls as the image of God. But they were not agreed on what quality made us this image. Like Merton, Descartes identified this image as our freedom: "Free will alone or liberty of choice causes me to know that I bear the image and similitude of God" (Med. IV).

[15]In *Either/Or* Kierkegaard wrote of his difficulty in making a commitment. He concluded that it is the earnestness with which one makes a choice that brings one "into immediate relation to the eternal Power" (E/O, II, 171). Both Merton and Kierkegaard believed one could make a commitment only in a divine encounter. Merton seemed to say that God's presence enables one to decide, while Kierkegaard suggests that the earnestness of the decision brings one to God. Both saw freedom as the ability to make a commitment. A commitment might seem like a non-freedom, but that is not how Merton, Kierkegaard and many other religious people have known it. St. Augustine asked God: "From what profound and secret depth was my free will suddenly called forth in a moment so that I could bow my neck to your easy yoke?" (*Confessions,* 184). Again the freedom came with the decision.

the divine Mercy. So Merton wrote often of the *Mercy* of God (mercy is not owed; it is not deserved). Merton discovered his own freedom in the "interaction of two freedoms," for encountering the Freedom of God led his own will to break free. So his freedom was the "reflection," the "signature," or the image of God: we are "the mirror that receives his image." Freedom comes to us in *response* to the Freedom we have found. The theology of Merton is distinctive in identifying God with Freedom: God "is Freedom;" we commune "with the Freedom;" the Holy Spirit "is Liberty itself" (NSC, 200; NM, 16, 131). Merton was delivered from the compulsions of the world by knowing divine Freedom. The divine image is dead in us until it discovers "the touch of God's ineffable Mercy" (NM, 76).

Self-love enables us to survive, so it is good. But it acts "by an inner compulsion rooted in the nature itself." Self-love—as rooted in nature—acts necessarily; so in loving ourselves we are not free. Self-love "is a principle of necessity, of compulsion" (R, 314). But when we come to know the disinterested love that God has for us, we are lifted "above the necessities of our nature." Meeting the freedom of Divine Love enables us to love as we have been loved, and then we can sacrifice ourselves. Learning of God's free gift delivers us from self-love and our natural compulsions (see Bailey, 183).

Merton told of being born into an alienated world, and he came to reflect this world. His own alienation was supported by the alienated society in which he lived. Many have told of human alienation. Marx claimed alienation was caused by religion, but Merton claimed the reverse: religion can deliver us from the alienation of the world (MZM, 272–273). Religion—in being impractical—draws one apart from the automatic behavior that dominates the world. In religion we meet the Freedom of God and discover we are made in his image, so "prayer is the truest guarantee of personal freedom" (HGL, 159). When we pray freedom is dealing with Freedom:

> . . . prayer is a real source of personal freedom in the midst of a world in which men are dominated by massive organizations and rigid institutions which seek only to exploit them for money and power. Far from being the cause of alienation,

true religion in spirit is a liberating force that helps man to find himself in God (HGL, 159).

God is present in all things *freely,* "not by nature but by gift" (HGL, 644). It is by encountering God's free presence that we are set free. "My freedom is not fully free when left to itself. It becomes so when it is brought into the right relation with the freedom of another" (NMI, 25). Since human freedom must come from an encounter with freedom, Merton saw prayer bringing us back from alienation to our true selves.

Merton's autobiography begins with a section titled "Prisoners' Base" and tells of a long purgation from bondage; it ends with a section titled "Sweet Savor of Liberty." The early part of the work tells of the world stamping him with its image. His autobiography ends with his discovery of freedom in the austerity of a monastery. In the beginning and in the end, his identity comes to him as an image: the image of the world that is imposed by violence and the image of God that is freely received. In each case his soul is reflecting what it has known; his soul is a mirror. It acts in response: we can call God "Father" only after He has called us "Son." Merton would urge us to stand free of our automatic responses to the world and come before God and learn we are made as His image. St. Paul had exhorted the people of Corinth in a similar way: "As we have born the likeness of the earthly, let us bear the likeness of the heavenly" (1Cor. 15:49). This passing from one likeness to the other, from the prisoners' base to the savor of liberty is the subject of *The Seven Storey Mountain*—and the central message of Merton.

Proud Structure, Humble Freedom

As a young monk Thomas Merton wrote, "In humility is the greatest freedom" (SC, 27). This simple thought would be the basis of his social thought. Merton believed that many problems in the modern world are caused by individuals seeking to escape the humble awareness of who they really are, so they identify with a social structure that makes them "someone." By associating themselves with an objective structure they gain an identity of sorts and might gain recognition, but the role they have assumed estranges them from a humble and simple truth. They have relinquished their freedom to attain a "place" in the world. The place acts to conceal their contingency and radical need. They have "established themselves," but in doing so they are part of "the enormous, obsessive, uncontrollable dynamic of fabrication designed to protect mere fictitious identities" (RU, 15). They are then committed to defend the structure, for the structure gives them the only identity they can recognize. But the structure will support them only as long as they conform, so they become impersonal functions. As such, they feel "necessary" and "important," but necessity alienates them from their freedom. They are unwilling to allow it is "a very great thing to be little, which is to say: to be ourselves" (NMI, 122). They have arranged things so that they do not have to make "the ultimate and humble discovery of inner freedom" (Z, 46).

Through society we gain an exterior identity; it is like a passport photo. Then, instead of asking who we are, we adopt the identity that others can recognize. But Merton asks if one really exists because one's face is recognized, or because one's name has been included in *Who's Who?* and whether having one's picture in the Sunday paper is any sure indication that one is not a zombie? (NM, 74). We have sacrificed our true identity to be part of the larger picture. And while we live in "a world of collective illusion, our freedom remains abortive" (RU, 16-17).

In earlier days rural life allowed people a large measure of personal freedom. But now people have moved to the imposing city; "the city is the place where the mythology of power and war develop, the center from which the magic of power reaches out." "The city lives on its own myths." We sacrifice ourselves to enter the pace of urban culture and share in its mystique. And America is "the most advanced of all urban cultures" (CGB, 138). In many such passages Merton speaks of society involving a mythology, a mystique, a superstition, a magic power that takes us out of ourselves and makes us "significant," for we are part of a significant structure. Merton became known for his denunciations of modern life ("that empty temple full of dust and rubbish," "my own disgusting century," etc.). These phrases are from *The Seven Storey Mountain,* but comparable phrases continued throughout his writing. Yet this is not the total picture. He softened this perspective by making a distinction:

> I have been taken to task for yelling so loud that this is a perverse generation and no doubt I have put a lot of my own frustration into the cries: the *people* of the generation are good, so good, so helpless, some of them: the culture, the generation, is perverse and I see little hope for it. Why? Because by its very essence it is against Christ (HGL, 14; emphasis added).

Thus the "century," the "culture," or the "generation" is perverse, and the trouble is that free people identify with the culture and this is their downfall. They have identified with the times, and are drawn into the general momentum of events wherein their freedom is lost.

Merton hoped his own writing might liberate people by speaking to them apart from their social identity. He began to denounce all structures and systems whether they be the U.S. Government, the Catholic Church, or his own monastery: "all the systems are in the same boat." He warned about being a cog in a totalitarian machine, and added, "or in a religious one either." The contemplation is not a cog, for the contemplative is free. The contemplative is an "outlaw"—as was St. Paul. Merton liked to think of himself as "a sort of Christian anarchist" (RU, 14; HGL, 139, 458).

Merton knew he was part of a powerful Church and an international monastic order, and he feared thereby that he was contributing to the general delusion (HGL, 139). He would urge that "a mass religion of faceless ones" is no religion at all, for it only "delivers men over to the demons" (CGB, 82). He claimed that the United States was caught in a "political vertigo" that is "demonic" in origin (HGL, 161). Even monks can become "'demonized' by being incorporated into the power structure" (HGL, 504). They have "a magic idea of the contemplative life" and think that by following a rule and living a routine they will automatically become contemplatives. But this is using a monastic routine to evade a call to freedom.

Merton read an account of the protest march that Gandhi led against the salt works in India, and even there he feared lest individuals were lost in the mass movement. "Was it . . . completely and maturely personal, or did they in fact move as a mass, impelled by the will of a leader?" (HGL, 165). If they acted only as a group, their deeds were not free. Even when one says, "I think," it is often not the individual thinking at all, but the anonymous collectivity thinking for one (TMDP, 115). Merton was suspicious of any group action. He would see significance in the fact that the Old Covenant was made with a group, the "chosen people"—in remaining part of the group they remained part of the covenant. While the New Covenant is addressed to the individual: "If any*one* would come after me. . . ." Merton would modify the New Testament to read: "Masses indeed may be called, but only individuals are chosen" (DQ, 104).

Merton saw the secular world filled with philanthropists who identify with lofty ideals. They think better of themselves because of their ideals, yet they have "no love, only principles, only reasons" (MAG, 35). He even questioned the way Christian ethics appeals so strongly to the *natural law.* For Merton, the law is general and abstract, while Christianity is centered on the person. Persons can be known only as individuals; they cannot be contained by concepts. They are known only as individuals in love, and love requires that we must freely respond to each of them. Christian theology has argued in terms of human nature, and that is its danger. For nature can readily become a big hypostasis for the anonymous crowd (HGL, 141, 315). Grace is not an abstract quality; it is an event, an encounter with God (MZM, 277).

Merton believed the world was filled with political and social mystiques of all sorts, with "the mystifications of bureaucracy, communism and the police." As mass movements they take one outside of one's self and so offer an "ersatz of spirituality," but they are delusions, for "the masses" are always impersonal; they can have no spirituality for those who are part of them are not free (CWA, 105). The true mystic cannot be part of any mystique, political mysticism, or mass movement, for the activity of the mystic is centered upon the humble acceptance of freedom. To have any spirituality, a free individual must accept one's own fragile reality and assume responsibility for all one does.

Whenever one takes on a social role some freedom is renounced; the role acts to mechanize us. We become like the
machines we have made. He would advise that we try not to
work among machines (NSC, 86). And the negative imagery of
technology and the machine runs through the prose of Merton.
All "progress in technological culture" is a "progress in servility" (CGB, 308). We lose our selves in "the big slide into tech-
nical totalism." We fall into a "mechanical conformity to the
standards and prejudices of those around us, or for that matter, of mechanical and compulsive revolt against them" (CS,
1984, vol. xix, 75). We become "a mere cog in the totalitarian
machine," or "lost in the wheels of a social machine," or caught
in "the automatic mechanisms of collective life" (TS, 12; NSC,
53; DQ, 159). We no longer want to freely decide; we want to
be carried away by "the mechanisms of natural instincts," by
the "automatic response." Even our controversies are no
longer personal disagreements, they are impersonal arguments
between machines (CGL, 269). The technology of war has
taken over our decision to go to war, and wars proceed with a
momentum of their own:

> For now it is the weapons themselves that make all the de-
> cisions: men humbly obey the creations of their own technol-
> ogy. I wonder if a few of us may persuade our fellows to
> retain at least enough freedom to use machines instead of
> being used by them (HGL, 621).

Yet Merton would see the industrial world dominated by the
myth that we are making tremendous choices. But *we* are not
making decisions at all; decisions are "engineered" for us. We
have become passive, confused, ineffectual, and we are dominated by mindless routines that might lead us to nuclear war.
Should that war begin, it would all be automatic and no one to
blame. Each simply would have continued the mindless routine as nuclear war would overtake us. For we are possessed by
demons and "driven to ruinous adventures by technological
pride" (VC, 112).

The Church is supposed to be our way of liberation, yet even
it can act as "a social mechanism for self-justification," "a perfect and faultless machine for declaring itself not guilty," "a
machine for setting the unquiet conscience at rest," "a per-

fectly efficient machine for the manufacture of self-complacency," "a machine for excusing sin" (CGB, 116). The imagery
is repetitious, but the machine is the perfect symbol for any act
that is not free. The Church is the great hope for alienated ones
to recover their true identity, but the Church can also go along
with the system and tranquilize the faithful and "canonize the
hubris of technological society" (MZM, 275).

Even monasteries can be "mechanized," "spiritual dyna-
moes," "institutional machines," places of "monastic totalitarianism" that function by "legal clockwork." God is seen to be
above it all acting as "supreme Engineer" (CWA, 174), while
superiors are to see that "the machine is well oiled," and the
spiritual director is "a machine for producing answers that will
work" (SDM, 10). Then the monks can "let themselves become
machines," "automatons praising God like machines" (SL,
118; MJ, 79, 50). Each monk is "a submissive cog" in "a machine for doing penance" (SL, 54). And looking back at Christian history, Merton wondered if many of the saints were nothing but "pious robots" (SJ, 133).

Today technological culture has provided us with enormous
power, but it has also given us the model by which we know
ourselves. We see no value in anything that is impractical and
this gives us a completely servile understanding of ourselves:
we are identified by our job, and "are so obsessed with *doing*
that we have no time and no imagination left for *being*" (CGB,
308). We have been reduced to our function, and this is the servile and alienated condition that makes American society. One
can no longer enjoy life, for human value is determined by production goals. Should one want to "have fun," the fun must
have a purpose. It must make us feel better and function better;
it must help us work better and "get ahead." "Fun" is no longer
spontaneous or gratuitous; it is useful. We even console ourselves that buying the equipment of fun will aid the economy.
Soon "having fun" becomes one more duty, part of our
productivity. But in trying to have fun we feel caught in a phony
spontaneity and feel guilt for losing a real spontaneity (a freedom) that we can no longer find. We look for our identity in
our actions as in a mirror, and the only actions we see are the
mindless and automatic deeds by which we conform. We see
only the acts by which we obey the "demands of life."

In American culture the most damaging machine is the propaganda machine; it is "a huge machine for lying;" it is "the machinery of alienation." When we were infants, we made our own "free cries." But in learning to speak, we learned to say what was expected and began to conform. We adopted the cliches of our society, and each cliche includes an automatic pattern of behavior. In learning a language the child takes on the "demands" of culture, for there comes "with words themselves a kind of servitude" (CGB, 99). The child soon becomes involved in "public relations" and uses language to "engineer consent." Propaganda has taken over the child's mind; it will enable the child to go places. Public opinion takes care of the rest.

Propaganda "makes up our mind for us," yet we continue to think we are free. But propaganda is originated by no one; "it is the mass mind, the general 'they,' the anonymous whole." Since "everyone" agrees, how could anyone be wrong? The result is a society of frantic activity surrounding a "massive inertia" of spirit, a process sustained by "the repetition of statements and slogans without meaning." The phrases and slogans have been tailored to run mechanically through our mind till we cannot distinguish the true from the false. We live in a dream world and feel vaguely threatened by alien dreamers. We act as we are told to act. But "we do not know ourselves or our adversaries. We are myths to ourselves and they are myths to us" (HGL, 446). Mythologies come into conflict, and soon mythologies will be at war. Vast impersonal structures will be in conflict and many humble freedoms will be killed. Still people are unwilling to renounce the structures that give them their identities. They die for a cause and consider it noble as if causes were of greater value than people. And they do not even feel guilty, for they are all part of "the great formless sea of irresponsibility." In the mass each individual is insulated from one's self and all others by layers of insensibility.

> Each individual in the mass . . . doesn't care, he doesn't hear, he doesn't think. He does not act, he is pushed. He does not talk, he produces conventional sounds when stimulated by the appropriate noises. He does not think, he secretes cliches (NSC, 55).

We have become addicted "to the kind of narcotic thinking induced by the mass media." We have become zombies, dead bodies moved by evil spirits, "demonized," alienated from the freedom that was ours. Perhaps we become aware of the sham around us and within us and ask how we can escape from the pervasive deluge of falsehood. We cannot distinguish between the false and the true, for "we are flooded, carried away with tidal waves of judgment, opinion, analysis" (CGB, 191). "With the mental bombardment everybody lives under, it is just not possible to see straight" (HGL, 295). We want to break free, but we do not know where to begin.

For Merton deliverance comes primarily through religion— and to some extent through art. Both of these offer ways of seeing the world apart from how it might be used. So religion and art are dismissed by the technological world as activities of no consequence. But it will be through acts of no consequence that we can recover our freedom. In religion we come before God and this frees us from the domination of technology, but in order to come before God we must step aside from the illusion of power that social structures have given us. We must accept the freedom of being no one.

Since nature is a mechanical process, Merton would see our freedom in the supernatural order (NMI, 192). Real religious belief can liberate us from the mechanisms that are less than human (CGB, 88). Merton told of finding his own freedom in coming to Catholicism. But he believed that Protestants can find their freedom in a similar way. He would tell of the other great religions guaranteeing a similar freedom. The Jews had received the promise to Abraham as "a promise of freedom" from the slavery of Egypt and a call to enter the "liberty of the people of God." In Islam there is "a freedom which lifts the believer above the limitations dictated by nature, by race, by society." While Muslims speak of God as the compassionate and the merciful, Merton would ask, "What are compassion and mercy but the gifts of freedom to freedom?" So too the Oriental religions "aim ultimately at liberation from the unending natural round, at freedom of spirit;" they give one "a principle of liberty" by which one can rise above necessity and process (CGB, 90). But irreligion and the political pseudo-religions and social mystiques and the superstitions of totalitarianism do the opposite. They make us slaves, sick to the core of our being: they have robbed us of our freedom and "made man a machine for his own destruction" (CGB, 91). But we escape from mechanized slavery by coming to religion, for in the truly religious moment we are

> Freedom from domination, freedom to live one's own spiritual life, freedom to seek the highest truth, unabashed by any human pressure or any collective demand, the ability to say one's own "yes" and one's own "no" and not merely to echo the "yes" or "no" of state, party, corporation, army or system. This is inseparable from authentic religion (CGB, 91).

But the artist offers a similar way of deliverance, but only the artist who refuses to be part of the propaganda machine. The artist will offer a personal vision apart from the mass opinion of the times and this personal vision can draw us back to our freedom. Artists will continue "to do what they know they must do, paint and write and create outside and against the officially subsidized culture." As such they will carry on their "disreputable, insolent, and prophetic diatribe" against all propaganda (CGB, 283). Some artists might sell out to the establishment. "The writer who submits to becoming 'an engineer of the soul' is in complicity with the secret police—or with the advertising business" (RU, 170). Others (like Buadelaire and Rimbaud) tried to break free of social convention only to pour out their energy in resisting tyrannical pressures; they came up with an anti-art, a reaction against society. Their art was a cry of protest against their society but it was dependent on their society, so their bondage remains. They are caught in the myth of art. Their art only establishes society more firmly in its complacent rejection. To be a true artist one must break with social pressures and discover one's freedom of conscience, and "this is a spiritual value and its roots are ultimately religious" (RU, 167). Again Merton is relating true art to true religion. "If there exists a kind of freedom that can be advanced by bad writing, I don't want any part of it" (MAG, 257).

The true poet has always seen life in its unpredictability, and this vision can allow others to open their eyes and see apart from the mindless media (RU, 159). And Merton would see his own work as both a religious man and artist as an effort to repeat a simple truth to our culture: the emperor is not wearing any clothes (RU, 62). It is a humiliating truth, but only by accepting it can the emperor and the enthusiastic crowd return to themselves, and there they could find their freedom. All poets are said to be monks (a radical reversal from earlier claims of poet and monk in conflict), for the poet acts outside the mystique of accepted categories—and so should the monk. It is the businessman, the propagandist, the politician, not the poet who believe in the "magic of words." The magic of words occurs when words are deliberately reduced to unintelligibility to make a mindless appeal to those unwilling to think; word magic is a trick to leave us under the spell of propaganda.

Merton feared that he had become part of the propaganda machine of Catholicism or that of monastic life. He told of not wanting to develop any personal following or lead a popular "movement" (HGL, 134). He was "nauseated" with causes, programs, ideals, and other abstract motivations. "Every definite program is now a deception, every precise plan is now a trap" (RU, 60). When some of his articles were not approved for publication, he was glad to have copies mimeographed for a small circle of friends. He found this to be "more meaningful because it lacks that mass, anonymous, stupefied quality that everything else has" (HGL, 204). Not long before his death he started a mimeographed magazine *Monk's Pond.* It would be "an enterprise of no account, with no money involved, to be given out free" (HGL, 635). This way he hoped to stand apart from the competing floods of propaganda that were carrying a perverse generation further from itself.

Merton believed that the people who live in the ghettos of America were more immune to propaganda than the rest of society. They have been rejected by the social machine. They have their own myths, but these are not transmitted to them from above. They arise from their own spontaneity. So Merton would conclude, "I am more and more convinced that the real people in this country are the Indians—and Negroes, etc." (HGL, 136). For these and the elderly and the chronically ill have no place in the productive machine; perhaps we do not even see them at all, but that frees them from the demands to be part of the system.

> We (society at large) have lost our sense of values and our vi-
> sion. We despise everything that Christ loves, everything
> marked with his compassion. We love fatness health bursting
> smiles the radiance of satisfied bodies all properly fed and
> rested and sated and washed and perfumed and sexually re-
> lieved. Everything else is a horror and a scandal to us. How
> sad (HGL, 138).

Merton believed that pride had become so deeply imbedded in
society that we share a common blindness. We have a "*hubris*
of affluence and power," and a "communion in arrogance"
(RU, 3). He visited the old people living at a home run by the
Little Sisters of the Poor in Louisville, and he concluded that
the "beautiful, beat, wrecked, almost helpless old people" are
the ones that Christ loves most. They were the forgotten ones,
the ones passed over by propaganda and production. Society
in its pride has overlooked them and left them behind; now
they can relate to God in humility and freedom.

The deeds of the social individual are automatic and his
thoughts are a confusion of public opinions. He lives the mystiques of his times and has no reason to question; he is proud
that he conforms to all that is expected. But maybe the words
of God or maybe the words of a poet might give him a vague
sense that another kind of living is possible. That is, one might
live apart from the common confusion and the mindless cliches
by which it is sustained. One's only assurance is the freedom
of God. Yet this is greater than any social compulsion.

Merton was annoyed that many of his fellow monks were
concerned that monasticism should "count" in the modern
world—this is precisely what monasticism must never do. And
the way the monk can avoid counting anywhere is to recognize
"the absolute primacy and necessity of silent, hidden, poor, apparently fruitless prayer" (HGL, 371). With a sense that our
prayer is producing nothing, we know we are free.

Journey to Freedom

Merton has told of two forms of slavery, one within and one
without, and both constitute the fallen world.

First, there is a slavery to our appetites, the impulse of the moment: we are dominated by the "compulsions and anxieties and weaknesses of a will left to itself." Our flesh and our passions "tend to anarchy," and we are responding "blindly and automatically to every stimulus that presents itself" (NM, 71). We are caught in an "awful pattern of lusts, greeds, angers and hatreds." To gain control of our lives we must discipline our appetites.

> No man who simply eats and drinks whenever he feels like eating and drinking, who smokes whenever he feels the urge to light a cigarette, who gratifies his curiosity and sensuality whenever they are stimulated, can consider himself a free person. He has renounced his spiritual freedom and become the servant of bodily impulse (NSC, 85).

Merton saw the first twenty years of his life as a slavery to his impulse; he was unable to commit himself to do what he wanted. This was treated in the first section of the present chapter.

Second, there is a slavery to the demands of society. Perhaps to discipline the appetites one joins a group. But then group conformity becomes a servitude. The young Merton knew he needed discipline. Shortly after his conversion he began writing a novel in which the central character reflected that priests are luckier than others: "For them, from now on, everything is definite, is settled for them." His own life seemed remote "from the kind of discipline" common in a seminary. He told of being "afraid of the discipline itself," but he seemed to believe it was just what he needed to gain self control. (A brief unfinished text in the archives of Bellarmine College.) The "common life" of the monastery was the way Merton would free himself from his appetites. "The whole purpose of the monastic life is to purify man's freedom from this 'stain' of servility" (SL, 24). He decided to leave "the world with its false freedom" and the "weakness of will" he had known (see SL, 25). But in the monastery Merton found a new form of slavery, slavery to the mystique of the group with which he identified. This communal slavery was treated in the previous section.

In being delivered from the domination of appetite, one can surrender oneself to the mechanical behavior of monastic life,

to "automatic obedience" (VC, 171). A mere outward conformity or even the formalistic participation in ceremonies of
collective worship can stifle our freedom and stunt our spiritual growth (NM, 131). Substituting cloister routines for
worldly routines can be an evasion of the call to authentic
inner freedom (CWA, 37). Merton continued to believe in the
discipline of monastic life, but he also knew it could become a
servitude. While teaching a course on St. Paul, he found it
became "practically a course in Christian liberty." He used passages of St. Paul that talk of servitude under the Law to tell of a
servitude in monastic practices. He warned that "formalism"
can mask itself as religion. This betrays what religion is about,
for the purpose of religion is liberation.

Thus "slavery" can take two forms: one can be a slave to appetites and passions, or one can be a slave to group pressures.
The first involves the weakening and stifling of "our being in
the confusion of fleshly license." The second "barricades itself
behind legalism and superstition." In either case the spirit is
enslaved, "whether its servitude be that of frank licentiousness
or of apparent severity" (NM, 134). These were the two forms
of bondage Merton wrote of and believed he had known.

People assume these servitudes because they want to find
their identity in their appetites or they want to find their identity in a structure. Unwilling to take personal responsibility for
one's self, one surrenders to appetites—and finds that "compulsions have reduced him to a shadow of a genuine person"
(NSC, 86). Another might surrender to the values of a group,
only to find he is reduced to being "a husk, a mask, a puppet"
(DQ, 106). The difficulty with both ways of "finding" an identity is that they are passive; they ignore that only one's free action can determine who one is. We can be ourselves only by our
choices. "It is our liberty that makes us persons" (NSC, 202).

Merton told of a moment of freedom as he knelt in the
Church of St. Francis Xavier and committed himself to the
priesthood, and told of another such moment as he rode
the train from upstate New York to the monastery of Gethsemani. But freedom is not something one can win once and for
ever; it is something that one must claim every moment. It
"must be recovered by long and patient struggle" (NM, 135).
And it was in terms of this ongoing struggle that Merton en-

tered the monastery and for twenty-seven years continued to believe in monastic life.

For Merton the exterior discipline of the monastery should free the monk from the day-to-day struggle of life so that he might deal with a more ultimate struggle. This is the struggle between life and death, a struggle that goes on in our flesh and emotions, but more so in our mind and spirit. When one lacks all group support one begins beating one's head against a wall of doubt, "a doubt that undermines his very reasons for existing and for doing what he does" (MJ, 206; DQ, 157). One is involved in a terrible wrestling "of being and nothingness, spirit and void." It is the most terrible of all wars and is "fought on the brink of infinite despair." The existential reality of one's own self is being questioned and nothing is assured beforehand. And the fundamental problem is that the issue of the struggle is "*left to our own choice*"—and that "constitutes the dark terror of the *agonia:* we cannot be sure of our own choice" (NM, 10). This is the freedom that we fear; this is why we conceal it under the "needs" of our body or the "needs" of social conformity. Yet at our personal center we do not find a "need," we do not find a "fact," we find a freedom. We must decide whether we will be and who we will be. This is the "existential freedom" that we try to avoid, but from time to time our automatic behavior is seen for what it is: an evasion, an effort to forget the doubt, inner struggle and responsibility that is at our center.

We are left to choose between a radical despair and a radical joy; it is a choice, for neither alternative is given as a fact. We are free. We finally see there is no necessity within (a compulsion) or without (a conformity) by which we can escape. Only our decision now and our ongoing decisions will make us who we are. So freedom "remains the object of our greatest anxiety. We strive to keep it hidden from ourselves precisely because the truth will make us free, and we prefer to be slaves." We fear taking responsibility for our own acts and for our identity (NM, 134).

Those immersed in a social structure can claim they are only doing what they "have to do," only what "anyone would have done." Society has decided for its members and absolves them of guilt. Society can do horrible things, and no one need feel guilty when it is over. Only society is responsible, and society is no one. For society is only "the mythical being which thinks and acts for everybody." And "those who take part in its acts can do so insofar as they have abstracted themselves from themselves and have surrendered to the public void" (MZM, 264). By identifying with the void, each member of society avoids the decision that is authentically one's own. Each is abstracted into the "general will," into the "universal noise." Members of a society "consent passively, they do not choose, they do not decide. They accept what has been decided by the public, that is by nobody."

The social will has determined what all should do, and if no one speaks against it, it will be easier for all. But at the moment one decides to act freely, the social fantasy disappears. Society is seen as a deceptive myth. But the one who sees this is left to deal with the weakness and hesitation that come from standing apart from the crowd. One confronts the humility of being only one's self.

> Decision begins with the acceptance of one's own finiteness, one's own limitations, in fact, one's own nothingness: but when one's own nothingness is seen as a matter of personal choice, of free acceptance, and not as part of the vast, formless void of the anonymous mass, it acquires a name, a presence, a voice, an option. . . . (MZM, 266).

We have descended into a depth wherein the social rules do not determine us, and we are confronted with our own weakness and the terrible choices that are ours. We have found beneath our busy activities "the ground of doubt and self-questioning which sooner or later must bring us face to face with the ultimate meaning of our life" (CP, 24). We must make an existential choice between all or nothing. The "conversion" asked of us by Christ is a turning away from social approval to a freedom based "on direct dependence on an invisible and inscrutable God, in pure faith" (CP, 25). That is, we are dangling free and exposed to "existential dread."

> When we are reduced to our last extreme, there is no further evasion. The choice is a terrible one. It is made in the heart of darkness, but with an intuition that is unbearable in its

angelic clarity: when we who have been destroyed and seem to be in hell miraculously choose God! (NMI, 208).

Merton sympathized with the existentialists and adopted some of their language (See VC, 23–24; RJ, 125). He knew that many existentialists did not believe in God, but he judged the majority of them did. He took up their call for authenticity and argued that this call is heard at the depths of one's conscience, and the very fact of having a conscience would be incomprehensible without a transcendent Ground of being, a God, to whom one might respond.

> Hence, the basic choice by which one elects to have one's own personal, autonomous existence is a choice *of oneself as a freedom that has been gratuitously given by God.* It is acceptance of one's existence and one's freedom as pure gift (MZM, 269; emphasis in the text).

Merton introduced one of his books by the claim it was for the solitary one who comes to "a moment of ultimate choice, in which he finds himself challenged in the roots of his own existence" (RU, 3). Only by facing this challenge apart from the pressures of the crowd does one come to a "mystical spontaneity," a spontaneity that "begins with the free option of faith;" "faith is a matter of freedom . . . the free receiving of a freely given grace" (NM, 134: TS, 13). Faith is not for the mass man, "the passive, inert man who drifts with the crowd and never decides anything for himself" (DQ, 104). The mass man can recite the Christian creed or some other creed, but this is not faith. Faith involves a free and personal appropriation of the free and personal God. Necessity, on the part of God or of ourselves, has nothing to do with faith or our deliverance. And that involves the humility of the believer. God does not owe us grace; he gives it in his mercy. And on our part we are not compelled to receive mercy. The believer becomes "aware of the fact that his ultimate fulfilment or destruction depend on his own free choice" (NM, 14). And this means fear and trembling.

The whole life of faith depends on a free call and a free response. Faith is the beginning of the way to mystical contemplation, but contemplation does not seize us and carry us away in rapture. It is a free response to what is freely offered ("one must first be called to this contemplative freedom" [DQ, 165]). Mystical contemplation is a pure gift of God. "God gives it to whom he wills, when he wills, and in the way and degree in which he wills" (FA, 105). And on our part "the eye which opens to his presence is . . . in the very heart of our freedom (TS, 51). This double freedom (God's and our own) is evident even in the highest graces of mystical union: There we meet God as an "abyss of *freedom*" and we can pass "utterly out of our own selfhood and into its own immensity of *liberty* and joy" (NSC, 227; emphasis added). And even salvation will be ours "only if it is freely received, as it is freely given" (NM, 28). The whole journey of faith has proceeded by one's own decisions. One is free to accept mercy, free to believe, free to contemplate, and free to enter eternal life. The whole of the Christian life is a grace. This gives us great confidence and great uncertainty. We would like to be lost in a system that would carry us along and guarantee salvation. But a system of any sort can never include ourselves, for we are a freedom. So apart from all law, system, necessity or justice, God comes to us with mercy. And apart from any law, system, necessity or justice, we can choose to respond. On our part, we can be grateful to God. The mercy of God and the gratitude of the human are constant themes in the writings of Merton. Neither mercy nor gratitude can be part of a system or natural law. They are in excess of what is required; they are personal terms with meaning only in the freedom of a personal exchange.

The natural world appears to proceed by its own rigid laws and our freedom is an emptiness that does not fit. So we try to escape the emptiness of subjectivity by surrendering to the power of objective law. We value the powerful drives (law of our appetite) that would carry us out of ourselves; we would then be only a "mechanical response." Then "the 'I' who regards itself as a purely isolated subject surrounded by objects also regards itself implicitly as an object. In a world where no one else, no 'other,' is willingly identified, the 'I' also loses its identity" (MZM, 268). In allowing no other freedom to exist, the "I" has become an object itself in a world of objects. The only inner reality it will recognize is the automatic impulse that seems objective. This was the helplessness Merton knew as a young man following his "natural appetites." But by his religious awakening, he came upon a freedom that was above the necessities of nature, and encountering a freedom he was able to freely respond. If all we know are things, we will "passively acquiesce" to becoming a thing. We become *images of the world* into which we are born—losing ourself in the mechanisms of the world and doing violence to our person. But beyond the determined world there is the divine freedom, and by our "response" to the God who is simply "there," we become *images of God,* and as God is personal we too become persons. The merciful presence of God has freed us from the automatic response.

Merton began his autobiography by saying he was both the image of the violent and selfish world into which he was born and the image of God. His life involved many unpredictable changes, but all that he did can be seen as a "long and patient struggle" to achieve his freedom as image of God.

Merton was resolutely theist throughout all the changes in his writing. He never softened this personal theism in reaching out to Zen Buddhists or other contemplative traditions reluctant to speak of a personal God. He could have softened his terms to speak more of the Ground of being, the Godhead, etc., but he did not. Even his closing prayer at the monastic conference in Calcutta was radically theist, though many of the attending monks were not (R, 512). Merton would apply the personal terms of Christianity (grace, mercy, love, etc.) to the Zen experience, though Zen Buddhists are notably unwilling to speak this way. Merton would write to Daisetz Suzuki, "With us this stress on freedom, God's freedom, the *indeterminateness* of salvation, is the thing that corresponds to Zen in Christianity" (HGL, 565). He would tell of "God's freedom" being at work outside of all set forms: the "Lord who speaks of freedom in the ground of our being still continues to speak to every man" (CGB, 326). We can hear the Lord's voice whether we are good or bad, wise or foolish, believers or not believers, for all is free. When we do hear God,

> . . . there is always this sudden irruption, this breakthrough of God's freedom into our life, turning the whole thing upside down so that it comes out, contrary to all expectation,

right side up. This is grace, this is salvation, this is Christianity. And, so far as I can see, it is also very much like Zen. And of course, personally, I like to see this freedom of God at work outside of all set forms, all rites, all theology, all contemplation—everything (HGL, 565).

Here Merton uses the language of Christian theism ("God's freedom," "grace") to interpret Zen and conclude they have much in common. He acknowledged that Zen has a "completely a-personal theodicy" (?) with "little or nothing said of love," but Merton suspected that "all the same some love (is) buried deep in Zen" (HGL, 441). But at times he asked himself if he was only projecting Christian experience into a Zen framework.[16] In a similar way he would claim that "Zen is the very atmosphere of the Gospels, and the Gospels are bursting with it" (HGL, 561). What is the basis of Merton's ongoing association of the Zen experience and its non-personal language with the Christian experience that is radically personal? The best answer would be to consider Merton's understanding of God as the freedom that sets us free; this God is in opposition to "the world" as a determined structure that makes us slaves. This freedom he found in Zen.

If one sees "the world" to be governed by an inevitable order, one might well identify God as the "Mind" of the universe. All things would then be ruled by a "cosmic justice," an all-encompassing order, and each individual would have a destiny or karma. But this arrangement would have nothing to do with the theology of Merton. For Merton the world is not ruled by justice, but by mercy.

> The world of consistency is the world of justice, but justice is not the final word. There is above the consistent and logical world of justice, an inconsistent illogical world where nothing "hangs together". . . . This inconsistent world is

---

[16]This passage ("some love buried deep in Zen") was written in January 1965, seven months after he had visited Suzuki in New York. Later Merton wrote of Suzuki's final words during their visit together: the "most important thing of all is love" (MZM, 41). Merton interpreted this as the sum of what Suzuki said or wrote! If these were the final words of Suzuki, it is surprising that Merton did not mention them in the letter of January 1965 when he was anxious to find some mention of love in Zen.

world is only consistent without God [handwritten annotation]

the realm of mercy. The world can only be "consistent" *without God.* His freedom will always threaten it with inconsistency—with unexpected gifts (RU, 31).

To become involved with a consistent world "is to submit to an obsession," and lose all freedom. But mercy breaks into the world of obsessions and overturns its apparent consistency. "Mercy is inconsistent," while law is consistent. Mercy "liberates from all the rigid and deterministic structures which magic strives to impose on reality (or which science, the child of magic, tries to impose)" (RU, 32; parenthesis in the text). The final phrase shows Merton's distaste for science, technology, and the machine; the earlier phrases bring out his distaste for system, law, and justice. But both distastes concern the image of a determined and predictable world. He tells us over and over the predictable world is not to be found. It is only the world of our imagining. He believed that we have become so obsessed with this artificial world that we value our humanity only insofar as we fit in an impersonal system. The impersonal process has been imposed on reality, while the Ultimate is free.

It is by our personal freedom that we transcend the world. And we can recognize other human beings by their freedoms, by the spontaneity by which they show themselves to be beyond any mechanical process. But Merton would see a similar spontaneity all around him in the world. ("Every wave of the sea is free. Every river on earth proclaims its own liberty. The independent trees own nothing" [SJ, 336]). For Merton this universal breakthrough of freedom testifies to a great Someone acting behind it all.

The Zen masters could well identify with the free character of all that is. To their disciples they would propose riddles and koans (the most famous would ask, "What is the sound of one hand clapping?"). These nonsensical koans would enable the Zen disciple to see the world itself apart from any "world view." For each world view imposes a structure on what is seen and an expectation of how it will behave. Eventually one sees only the "world view," what one expects to see—and one does not see the world. But one can be delivered from all views by meditating on the nonsense of a Zen koan; then one sees beyond the views to the waves, the rivers, and the trees as they are. They are free of the visions we impose on them. Freedom is everywhere; and the world is wonderfully inconsistent. Justice is not the law by which all things operate. It is an artificial structure imposed on things. It is the "magic" or the "myth" or the "science" by which we seek to avoid our own freedom and the freedom we encounter.

Merton expressed sympathy with all the great religious/ contemplative traditions: the Hassidic, the Sufi, the Tibetan, the Hindu, the American Indian, and, especially, the Zen Buddhist. But there was one contemplative tradition for which he regularly expressed distaste: Platonism/Neo-Platonism (SSM, 75; LL, 157; CWA, 63, 175; HGL, 580; AT, 14; RU, 161; FV, 114, 134; CP, 39; SCh, 149; see also CGB, 58). A tradition that had enormous influence on Christian monasticism. Why? Merton saw the Platonist contemplating the eternal essences of things, the changeless natures that could be studied rationally by science. Platonism is a system and its God is the great Geometer. While "our God is not a Platonist. Our Christian spirituality is not the intellectualism of Plotinus" (R, 413). Plato and Plotinus tell of an ultimate structure and an ultimate justice. For Merton, these are not ultimate at all. To make them ultimate is to deny the freedom that is. The other contemplative traditions lead one beyond necessity and structure. But there is no other tradition that tells so deeply of an ultimate freedom as Zen. For Merton an ultimate freedom means that Someone is behind it all. He found the free-spirit of the Zen monks testifying to the same gratuitous love that he found in the Gospels.

4

Others

The seed, by nature, waits to grow and bear
Fruit. Therefore it is not alone
As stones, or inanimate things are:
That is to say, alone by nature,
Or alone forever.

Merton believed that Christian faith leads one into a series of paradoxes. Three such paradoxes will be considered in the present Chapter: First, Solitude is not opposed to Society. For Merton found his movement into solitude enabled him to be in communion with people all around the world. Second, Contemplation is not opposed to Action. For Merton came to see contemplation is essential for anyone who would act apart from the general passivity. Third, Monasticism is not opposed to the concerns of a wider Society. For Merton believed his distant perspective on events enabled him to see better the needs of his fellow Americans. These paradoxes form the subsections of the present Chapter.

Solitude and Society

During his student days Merton was given to solitary walks; he told of camping alone when he was eighteen; he traveled alone across Europe and twice crossed the Atlantic alone: "the deepest happiness has always been when I was alone" (VC, 140, 141). While traveling alone to Cuba in April 1940, he noticed a church dedicated to La Solidad, Our Lady of Solitude. Going inside he saw a shadowed niche with a statue of the solitary Virgin; mindful of the communal demands of American life he observed, "One of my big devotions, and you never find her, never hear anything about her in this country" (SSM, 281).

Twenty months later and still seeking solitude, Merton became a Trappist monk, but he soon found the common life of the monastery intruded on his solitude. Then several years after he entered, many veterans of World War II came to the monastery, and Merton found "two hundred and seventy lovers of silence and solitude . . . packed into a building that was built for seventy." The intensity of communal living became increasingly difficult for him: it was far from what he was seeking in entering the monastery. God seemed to be calling him to go deeper into solitude, while the house in which he lived was "as crowded as a Paris street." When a minor illness brought him to a private room in the infirmary, he found his former ease with prayer returned. In community his prayer had become difficult, and he attributed the difficulty to his lack of solitude. *O beata solitudo,* he would write, *O sola beatitudo.* And in response God seemed to be telling his soul that eventually He would lead him to solitude. Then all created things would sear him so that he would fly from them in pain; he would ultimately be rejected, forgotten and abandoned by everyone. Then and only then would he find the solitude he desired; and then his solitude would bring fruit into the lives of people he had never known (SSM, 422).

In December of 1946—five years after entering the monastery—Merton informed his spiritual director that he wanted to transfer from the Cistercians to become either a Carthusian (a congregation of solitaries) or a hermit outright. He knew that at an earlier time the Cistercians had allowed some monks to become hermits, but in recent centuries this was no longer an option. So before he was allowed to take solemn vows as a Cistercian, Merton was required to renounce his hermit intentions. By his vows he committed himself to Cistercian "common life." Soon his solitude was further compromised when his autobiography brought him international fame, and the inner life of the solitary was public property. Events seemed to be moving him in a direction directly opposed to the solitude he was seeking. To understand his situation Merton identified with Jonah the prophet, for Jonah was thrown into the sea and transported in the belly of a whale to the place God would have him be. So Merton saw his own life: he was seeking solitude, but God seemed to be transporting him into a public role: "I found myself with an almost uncontrollable desire to go in the opposite direction. God pointed one way and all my ideals pointed in the other." Like Jonah, he was traveling towards his "destiny in the belly of a paradox" (SJ, 21).

Soon Merton was appointed instructor of scholastics, a somewhat public office within the monastery. But this gave him some opportunity for solitude and he felt drawn strongly to those who were the most solitary. Small adjustments were made for him in the monastic routine, but when an official Visitor came to the monastery and complained about the monks having a *"mentalité eremetique,"* that did it. Merton wrote to the Roman Congregation of Religious and asked permission to make a *transitus* to a Camaldolese monastery in Italy—a congregation of hermits. After some delay and considerable confusion, it was suggested that he first try to live the Trappist life as the other monks were doing, and that meant give up all contact with publishers and so forth for five years. He was told that, if at the end of that time he still wanted to make the *transitus,* his request would be regarded favorably.

While Merton was pressing his request for the hermit life, his abbot, with considerable difficulty, gained the approval from Cistercian authorities in Rome for Merton to live by himself in a fire-tower on the monastery property. But shortly after receiving this permission Merton surprised the abbot by renouncing the opportunity and volunteered to serve as novice director (TMM, Fox 151). As he began his new and public task he wrote to a friend: "I have made as much effort in that direction (solitude) as one can make without going beyond the limits of obedience" (SCh, 94). He stayed with the job for ten years and told of finding "a surprising amount of interior solitude among my novices." Through his "contact with other solitudes" he would revise some earlier outlooks. As novice director he took the novices out to the woods where he and they could walk alone.

In 1965 as Merton finished his term as novice director, he was allowed to move to a hermitage not far from the monastery. His first night there was October 12, 1964, but he was not

there fully until the following August. He felt relief: "Around
the community I am seldom in my right mind." But even then
he would return regularly for Mass and the noon meal. Shortly
after settling into his hermitage he wrote, "It seems that this
life I am now living is what I was really seeking when I entered
the monastery." Yet he continued to discover the meaning of
solitude: "I see more and more that solitude is not something
to play with. It is deadly serious, and much as I have wanted it,
I have not been serious enough about it" (VC, 154).

By the time he had moved to the hermitage he had developed
an immense correspondence, and visitors—expected and
unexpected—began streaming up to see him. In January 1968
a new abbot was elected and Merton was allowed considerable
freedom to travel. Soon one is left with a paradoxical image of
Merton's final solitude: abundant visitors, picnics near the
hermitage, an immense correspondence, frequent visits to
Louisville, and in his final year travels to New Mexico, Wash-
ington, D.C., California, Alaska, India, Ceylon, and Thailand.
Was this the solitude that Merton envisioned as he prayed in
Cuba at the church of La Solidad? Perhaps it was—for Merton
believed that solitude had a paradoxical quality: "the more we
are alone with God the more we are united with one another"
(SC, 33). In solitude we "find God—and find other men in
God" (SCh, 32). And God himself is "infinite solitude" and
"perfect society" (NSC, 68).

Merton believed the hermit was an essential part of the
Christian tradition. He identified with the early Christian
monks who went to the deserts of Egypt abandoning the secular society of their times, for they saw its tenets and values to
be "a shipwreck from which each single individual man had to
swim for his life" (WD, 3). In going to the desert the early
monk wanted to escape the false identity fabricated by society.
For the social self always involves some artifice (L&L, 35).
That is, human society demands a measure of pretense that
leaves one divided against one's self; so by leaving society each
monk sought a true identity. One became an anarchist of sorts.

Many early Christian writers believed the hermit embodied
the Christian ideal; when the Roman persecutions ended, the
hermits were considered successors of the martyrs (DQ, 131–
32). Merton studied the sources of Christian monasticism and

appealed to St. Benedict (the Benedictine Rule is the basis of Cistercian life) who allowed that some monks—after a long probation in the monastery—might be called to the hermit's life. Merton even claimed that the Benedictine Rule had an implicit orientation "towards eremitical solitude" (SL, 148).

Yet solitude can be found anywhere, even in the middle of a crowd. But when one is called to solitude, one wants to withdraw from society and let a physical distance express the spiritual distance one feels. Though some people have found solitude in the midst of worldly activities, Merton thought some physical solitude was morally necessary for contemplative prayer.

> There should be at least a room, or some corner where no one will find you and disturb you or notice you. You should be able to untether yourself from the world and set yourself free, loosing all the fine strings and strands of tension that bind you, by sight, by sound, by thought, to the presence of other men (SC, 52).

solitude [handwritten marginal note]

Yet true solitude is not physical; it is a spiritual abyss that opens in the center of the soul, an abyss created by a hunger that cannot be satisfied by any created thing. Responding to this hunger one will do all one can to avoid the amusements, noise, and business of society; one will avoid newspapers and magazines and not listen to the radio. "Keep your eyes clean and your ears quiet and your mind serene. Breath God's air. Work, if you can, under his sky" (SC, 54).

Yet there are dangers in the life of solitude. Many people have sought solitude simply because they cannot stand other people; but "it is dangerous to go into solitude merely because you like to be alone" (NSC, 79). Such people will not find solitude; they will find they have isolated themselves with a pack of devils. Others will seek solitude to act out the dreams of their own egos. These will not find solitude; they will only become eccentrics going their separate and erratic way. Others will adopt some form of regressive behavior: "what they want is not the desert but the womb" (DQ, 144). But in spite of these dangers, Merton believed there is a true vocation to solitude and that today both the world and the Church need solitaries more than ever. Why? Today powerful social groups are consuming persons by molding them into a shapeless and faceless mass. But the hermit will not conform.

Many people object to the hermit; they see solitude as only a form of escapism. But Merton believed the real "escapism" is found by burying oneself in the formless sea of irresponsibility that is the crowd, the mobs, the masses. By losing oneself in the "common opinion" one does not have to face the risk and the responsibility of true solitude; instead one lives the common life of the crowd with its diffuse, anonymous anxieties, its nameless fears and hostilities. In the crowd one is immersed in the meaninglessness of slogans to which one responds without thinking. One does not talk for oneself, one just produces conventional phrases when stimulated by an appropriate noise. This is the shipwreck from which each person must swim for one's life:

> to live in the midst of others, sharing nothing with them but the common noise and the general distraction, isolates a man in the worst way, separates him from reality in a way that is almost painless. It divides him off and separates him from other men and from his true self (NSC, 55).

This is how Merton saw the modern technological society and the world shaped by mass communications. In going apart one is leaving the isolation and mindless anonymity of mass living to make contact with one's true identity. One is trying to avoid the faceless identity of the crowd. Merton believed that it is only after a solitary discovery of one's true self that one can speak to others apart from the general noise. Then the listeners too might find themselves apart from the mindless noise. The solitary will disagree with those who believe self-deception and endless diversion is the way of truth. But in doing so the solitary will sweat blood in order to be loyal to God and to humanity as a whole, rather than to one of the idols offered by conflicting social structures. The solitary will leave "the mindless mind of Muzak and radio commercials" to find a humility and purity apart from the slogans and the gravitational pull that have alienated us from our self, from our God and from one another.

By going apart from the crowd the solitary discovers "that he and God are one: that God is alone as he himself is alone"

(DQ, 148). But Merton would not want such thoughts to be understood in the Neo-Platonic sense. (Plotinus had told of "the flight of the alone into the Alone." See Shannon, TMDP, 121.) In solitude one sees that one's duty is "to be faithful to solitude because in this way he is faithful to God." For the flight from one's true self is also the flight from God.

The true solitary is united with others because he or she is no longer entranced by the marginal concerns that dominate relationships today. The union is on a mystical level where one shares in the common human solitude apart from the diversions that alienate. But this is an explanation, and the solitary should not try to rationalize, defend or explain one's solitude, for the society of illusions will never understand those who do not conform. The Christian hermit will not be understood by other Christians, yet the Christian hermit is not really separated from the others: the hermit has a function within the Mystical Body of Christ. This function is the "paradoxical one of living outwardly separated" but spiritually united with the community. The solitary might feel that he or she is not good enough to share in the visible exercises of the community, then the solitary claims "some hidden function, in the community's spiritual cellar" (TS, 103). The hermit is a witness of the transcendent character of the Christian bond. The hermit reminds us to look beyond our natural obsession with the gregarious forms of Christian life and discover the mystical character of Christian unity. In the early days of the Church, when hermits filled the deserts of Egypt and Syria, they were admired—not for their asceticism—but for their charity and discretion. They had despaired of social illusions, so they became a sign of love and hope for the Christian people living in the towns. By their charity they testified to "the spiritual and mystical character of the Christian Church." For they showed that the Christian hermit can "paradoxically live even closer to the heart of the Church than one who is in the midst of her apostolic activities" (DQ, 149). When Merton was tempted to renounce his monastic life he reminded himself: "This is a gift (his vocation to solitude) not for myself, but for everyone" (Griffin, 108).

Today, when the world seems to have "become one immense and idiotic fiction, and when the virus of mendacity creeps into every vein and organ of the social body," the only healthy reaction is some form of protest. "In a totalitarian world, there is need before all else of hermits." Today, hermits are more necessary than martyrs. Yet hermits and martyrs have something in common: both have despaired of conventional and fictitious values to trust in the mercy of God. The hermits have withdrawn to the healing silence of the wilderness "to heal in themselves the wounds of the entire world."

Merton would have it that the door to solitude cannot be forced and it opens only from the inside (DQ, 152). But the one who freely passes through this door "falls into the desert the way ripe fruit falls out of a tree" (DQ, 153). But the one living apart from social conventions finds there is no common myth to justify one's deeds, and this fills one with terror. Many who flee mass society will take refuge in some marginal group that will give them a measure of social support. But others remain strangers wherever they go. They are the ones with a really important place "in a world like ours that has degraded the human person and lost all respect for that awesome loneliness in which each single spirit must confront the living God" (DQ, 154). The importance of the hermit lies in the fact that he or she has taken a place that society disdains. In being neglected by others one can better confront the living God.

In living without social support one finds poverty "invades his soul as well as his body." The poverty is so great "that he does not even see God," but only because God is not far enough away to be seen as an object. Those who live in society can find "the will of God" through their social obligations. But free of social obligations one receives the will of God without words or human comprehension; the will of God becomes a baffling and incomprehensible mystery that the solitary must interpret for oneself.

In some sense the solitary shares in the solitude of God; that is, like God he too transcends the world. So the world resents God and resents the solitary; for the solitary in his isolation and God in his transcendence refuse to be caught in slogans and worldly enthusiasms. Since "society" can never meet the transcendent God, it invents immanent gods more to its liking. The hermit transcends society and thus reminds society of the false god it is serving. The silent presence of the solitary tells worldly people, in ways they can barely understand, that "if

they were able to discover and appreciate their own inner solitude they would immediately discover God" (DQ, 158). So the
solitary and the transcendent God are more than society can
allow. Merton claimed that even Christian believers can develop a "god" that is less the God of faith and more the product
of a religious and social routine. This god protects the members of society from a deep encounter between the true self and
the true God (L&L, 37).

In society each person has a social image, an image Merton
saw made largely of prejudice, posturing and pharisaic self-
concern. Only in leaving that image can one discover the deep
self of solitude and love. This is a silent self

> whose presence is disturbing precisely because it is so silent;
> it *can't* be spoken. It has to remain silent. To articulate it, to
> verbalize it, is to tamper with it, and in some ways to destroy
> it (L&L, 36).

But in discovering this secret self one discovers a great paradox: "This inner 'I,' who is always alone, is always universal."
For whenever I enter this inmost 'I,' my own solitude meets the
solitude of God and the solitude of every other human. It is a
union beyond division, beyond limitation, and beyond selfish
affirmation. By withdrawing from the fictional identity developed in society one finds one's self "on the level of a more perfect spiritual society" (SJ, 262). This is the deeper spiritual
identity we have within. This common identity influenced the
way Merton hoped to write:

> I seek to speak to you, in some way, as your own self. Who
> can tell what this may mean? I myself do not know. But if you
> listen, things will be said that are perhaps not written in this
> book. And this will be due not to me, but to One who lives
> and speaks in both (HR, 67).

Official prose is written by no one and it is addressed to no
one; it is the voice of the crowd—the voice of the common illusion. Yet many people fight to gain a place within the illusion
and hope their names will be prominent in the general deluge
of words. But the one who so understands one's identity can
never hear God, for God is personal and speaks only to the person. When caught in the torrent of talk, one can hear no one,

human or divine. So each of us must leave the crowd and come to the silence wherein one can learn to listen and speak. There we can find the truth that unites us instead of the pseudo union of the crowd. There "we can find ourself engulfed in such happiness that it cannot be explained: the happiness of being at one with everything in that hidden ground of Love for which there can be no explanations" (HGL, 115). Only apart from the faceless crowd does it make sense to speak of love at all. So Merton rejoiced in the solitude of his final years: "Living alone in the woods, I am more appreciative of friendship than ever before" (HGL, 116). Solitude makes friendship possible. For "the solitary, far from enclosing himself in himself, becomes everyman" (RU, 18). This is the paradox: "There is One Solitude in which all persons are at once together and alone" (L&L, 15). To have a friend is not to interfere with the other's solitude. Friends will not lose themselves in the common noise, for friendships are between persons. And one is "a person insofar as he has a secret and is a solitude of his own that cannot be communicated to anyone else" (NMI, 244). We may speak to each other, but then we can also know that more is involved than our own voices: "When 'I' enter into a dialogue with 'you' and each of us knows who is speaking, it turns out that we are both Christ" (HGL, 387). Then a single voice seems to rise from our common depths: "It is the Lord." "For Christ speaks in us only when we speak as men to one another and not as members of something, officials, or what have you" (HGL, 385).[17]

Eventually Merton insisted on speaking on his own and not as an official voice of his Church or his monastery (even as late as the mid 1950s he had wanted to speak only "as the mouthpiece of a tradition centuries old." See SL, xii). He came to believe that, if he spoke simply of his own experience apart from any group allegiance, other solitudes would understand. Yet people kept asking him "Whom do you represent? What religion do you represent?" And he did not want to answer (AJ,

---

[17]Merton's notebooks reveal a strong sense of failure that he had never developed a really intimate relationship (Bailey, 28; Cashen, 12). Concerned about never having such a friend he asked to visit a psychiatrist in Louisville who assured him that he had an exceptional capacity to relate to others (Furlong, 234).

305). His task was to be "the solitary explorer" who would not jump on the latest bandwagons, but would "search the existential depths of faith in its silences, its ambiguities, and in those certainties which lie deeper than the bottom of anxiety." On this level "the division between Believer and Unbeliever ceases to be so crystal clear" (FV, 213). This was the level on which he was called to live. In solitude he wanted to realize his brotherhood with the non-Christian monks of the East (HGL, 648). He would speak with them of what they had found in solitude.

> Ecumenism seeks the inner and ultimate spiritual "ground" which underlies all articulated differences. A genuinely fruitful dialogue cannot be content with a polite diplomatic interest in other religions and their beliefs. It seeks a deeper level, on which religious traditions have always claimed to bear witness to a higher and more personal knowledge of God than that which is contained simply in exterior worship and formulated doctrine (MZM, 204).

His correspondence became an ecumenical dialogue that was apart from the official stances affirmed by the different creeds, for these could become phrases that belonged to no one. He brought practitioners of Raja Yoga, Zen, Hasidism, Tibetan Buddhism, and Sufism to his monastery. He sponsored small gatherings at his hermitage and wrote personal letters to a wide array of people, religious and non-religious. In Calcutta he spoke to monks of many traditions and asked them to go "beyond their own words and their own understanding in the silence of an ultimate experience" (AJ, 315). Yet he did not believe monks from different religious traditions should form a common community, as some were then suggesting (AJ, 85, 173). When he asked the Tibetan monks what they thought of his desire for radical solitude, he seemed surprised that all the rimpoches were opposed to absolute solitude (AJ, 103). In 1963 Merton tried to sum up his basic message:

> Whatever I may have written, I think it can all be reduced in the end to this one root truth: that God calls human persons to union with himself and with one another in Christ, in the Church which is his Mystical Body (Mott, SMTM, 392).

Thus the solitary is the one who has renounced the myth of social unity through diversion "in order to attain to union on a higher and more spiritual level of the Body of Christ" (DQ, 142).

Even when Merton was making his decision to enter the Trappists he had claimed that anyone "who believes in the Mystical Body of Christ" could understand that the Trappist assists one's fellow Christian (SecJ, 222). A few weeks later he was appealing to the Mystical Body when he wrote to his friends to explain his decision; again he appealed to the Mystical Body to tell of his life (RJ, 168). References to the Mystical Body run through many works: *The Seven Storey Mountain* claimed that every song and prayer of the monks was "with Christ in His Mystical Body" (SSM, 379). *The Seeds of Contemplation* has chapter headings which claim, "We are One Man" with "A Body of Broken Bones;" and to become Christ is to enter the life of the Mystical Body (SC, 88). He explained the title of *No Man is an Island:* "The reference is to the Mystical Body" (RJ, 216). This Body is the Church, but this Body is not properly an organization; it is an organism (DQ, 111). It is a living thing in which members are one in a "union that comes from the consciousness of individual fallibility and poverty" (DQ, 110). It is a society based on freedom and love and the unity found in Christ, the "hidden ground of Love." The Christian solitary does not renounce the Christian community, only the crowd that prohibits all community and makes people into "members of a many-headed beast" (SL, 43).

A Christian community is composed of those determined to avoid the images of power that society has taught them to project. The only people who can become "a genuine community of persons" are those who have first of all accepted their own fragile lot (MZM, 266). The community then formed would be based on "the solitude of the person who must think and decide for oneself without the warm support of collective fictions." But in accepting their common solitude and common need for the mercy of God, they no longer feel compelled to alienate themselves into a social image. Their alienation is ended and community is possible: it is "only when each man is one that mankind will once again become 'One';" we will

have attained the unity which makes "all men 'One Man'"
(DQ, 142).

Jesus has told us that we must lose our selves for His sake in
order to find our selves; so there is a losing-and-finding of self
integral to Christian spirituality. For Merton the self that we
must lose is the fictional identity. This self knows itself by the
role it plays in the anonymous mass; this self is what the solitary must lose—but only to find the true self in God. But, just
as one must lose the fictional self, so one must lose the fictional
society. But once again the loss is not final: one loses the anonymous crowd in order to find community in Christ. The hermit reminds us that the whole impersonal world is an illusion
that must be lost. So we fear the hermit and many Christians
feel uncomfortable with the claim that there are "Christian
hermits," for we fear losing our social identity, our common
label. Yet the hermit does not renounce community, the hermit
renounces only the mindless throng in order to discover humanity in the ultimate ground of love. The hermit going to the
desert renounces the artificial things of the city, to discover the
true world. The hermit renounces all things (self, society and
the world) in order to find these in their truth.

The hermits of the early Church brought about a vast social
change. For they reminded those in the city that the social roles
(master, slave, etc.) by which civil power was sustained were
not ultimate. This is the message that the hermit has for today:
the power of consumer society (a power that isolates us in a
wasteland more dreadful than that of any desert) is not ultimate. Only by renouncing consumer society and the illusions it
maintains can we begin to form a community in Christ.

Merton has identified with Jonah, for Jonah found God was
bringing him in a direction he did not intend to go. This is the
solitude of Merton: the more he intended to move into solitude, the more he believed Christ was drawing him into union
with all humanity. The more he tried to tell of himself, the
more Christ was showing him he would never be other than a
solitude (SJ, 229). The more he renounced possessions, the
more he discovered things in their truth. The more he renounced the superficiality of social gatherings, the more
deeply others became his friends.

Action and Contemplation

Merton believed the pace of American life had left Americans busier than ever, yet he found them helpless, passive and unable to act. They were made for contemplation, their highest and freest activity. But feeling incapable of this, a guilt was driving them "to seek oblivion in exterior motion," a constant agitation to keep their "spirit pleasantly numb" (AT, 24). He believed Americans were caught in a "total activism," a "frantic activity," "a demonic activism, a frenzy," a "breathless dynamism of the ephemeral." People work a sixty-hour week and complain they are the victims of modern life. They have no time to do what they want to do. Technology has given them great control over the physical world, but their technology makes demands that they must fulfill. They are controlled by events, and real decisions are made elsewhere. Their "acts" are mechanical responses to the "demands" of the times: they do what has to be done! They make the automatic movements with little sense of making free choices. Merton found widespread alienation in America and defined it as people imprisoned by something over which they have no control (CWA, 361; FV, 54). People have become "functionaries" of a power structure that uses them. A slave is alienated, for he does not act for himself. He might keep busy, but he remains "numb, inert and hopeless" for his free decisions do not count. Merton believed many Americans had become slaves, and contemplation would give them control over their lives.

Today people speak of the controlling force of history; it seems to define them and determine their deeds. While contemplation could take them apart from "history" into eternity and freedom—and there, apart from the compulsive world, they could discover their freedom to act. This will enable them to *make* history, and not have it make them. Merton calls on us to "renounce our fatalistic submission to economic and social forces, and give up the unquestioning belief in machines and processes which characterize the mass mind. History is ours to make." Today our primary task is to "try to recover our freedom, our moral autonomy, our capacity to control the forces that make for life and death in our society" (NA, 79, 16). But instead of assuming this control we tend "by our very passivity and fatalism to cooperate with the destructive forces that are leading inexorably to war" (See Powaski, 79). Our military "policy is dictated by the weapons themselves;" and both sides of a cold war passively await a mutual destruction that neither side intends or chooses (BP, 8). War seems inevitable; yet if we discover our freedom, we can avoid all such inevitability. Christian faith should remind us that life is not a fatality to which we must submit; it is a reality which we are called to shape.

Merton saw the political leaders of World War II dominated by events they should have directed:

> . . . they seemed to be the powerless victims of a social dy-
> namic that they were able neither to control nor to under-
> stand. They never seemed to dominate events, only to rush
> breathlessly after the parade of cataclysms, explaining why
> these had happened, and not aware of how they themselves
> had helped precipitate the worst of disasters (SD, 157–58).

The leaders were so "caught up" in the task of the day that they never saw the total picture. Gandhi lived during this period, but he had a different sense of life. He spent one day each week in contemplation, and this enabled him to shape events as a free man.

People are not free whenever their minds are possessed by ideas they have been given and never freely accepted. Someone else (often the mass media) has prescribed set phrases by which they act. Often they cannot recognize who has made their decisions; they simply do what seems to be expected. Many are so alienated without realizing it (TMA, 75). They are drawn passively into the current movement; and "the trouble with movements is that they sweep you off your feet and carry you away with the tide of activism" (HGL, 266). People even feel good as they "get involved" and make the necessary moves—they are carried along by events; the general activity frees everyone from responsibility. Only the crowd is acting and no one need feel guilty. Nations make war on other nations, but it is all "abstract, corporate, businesslike, cool, free of guilt-feelings" (FV, 7). "The enemy," "they," are responsible, and we are the victims! Merton repeatedly asked people to come apart from all

but that's what led to the success of the Civil rts. Movement

mass movements. "Stand on your own two feet"; that is, act freely and accept responsibility for all that you do.

Today in America we have made a fetish out of action, but that does not mean our free wills are active at all. In our ceaseless activity we have lost the ability to will anything (HR, 85; NM, 72). We have become zombies or puppets, pulled here and there by authorities we cannot identify. Currents of popular opinion act for us (HGL, 200); we are moving fast, but we are passive.

There seems to be an undefinable guilt for the freedom we have lost. We resent our situation. And resentment enables us to survive the general absurdity. But what is resentment? It is the last-ditch stand of freedom in a confused and compulsive world. "The confusion is inescapable, but at least we can refuse to accept it, we can say 'No.' We can live in a state of mute protest" (NSC, 108). Resentment may make the situation livable, but it can never make it healthy. From time to time the resentment breaks out in rage and uncontrolled violence. And the violence on the streets of America is only our repressed and helpless freedom crying out that it is still there.

Today conversations have become automatic; people say what they are expected to say and talk endlessly of pseudo-events. They have so often given voice to what "everyone" says, that they no longer know what they themselves think. Merton tells of entering the monastery "in revolt against the meaningless confusion of a life in which there was so much activity, so much movement . . . that I could not remember who I was" (HGL, 156). He wanted to discover a silence wherein he could know himself and learn to speak in a new way—a way that had nothing to do with popular currents of partisan propaganda (MAG, 188, 257). He was seeking a refuge from the busy activity of life and endless verbal assaults.[18]

Contemplation is rest—and that tells of a central difficulty people today have in trying to contemplate. Their minds are unable to stop; their mental activity has become compulsive.

---

[18]Even as a monk Merton would complain that his monastery was hyper-active: it is "like a munitions factory under wartime conditions of production." The monks head out to work "like a college football team taking the field," and so forth (R, 185).

Contemplation requires that they quiet down; for "contemplation means rest, suspension of activity, withdrawal into the mysterious inner solitude." Contemplation brings "rest from labor and surcease from interior activity" (SSM, 415; TMSB, 55). The extent of contemplative quiet can be seen by the Latin terms by which the Church Fathers spoke of it: contemplation was called *"quies," "otium," "vacatio,"* and even *"sancta dormitio"* ("rest," "leisure," "idleness," "holy sleep"; TMSB, 52, 53). Some Fathers believed that even a minimal bodily activity could be an impediment to contemplation (TMSB, 54). But the quiet should go beyond the body to a stillness of spirit. When contemplation has achieved the state of perfect union, the soul would be unable to act even if it should want to (TMSB, 53). This is the stillness we must discover, if ever we would act as ourselves.

The quiet of the contemplative life was often set in contrast with the work of the active life, and in the religious texts of the Middle Ages the contemplative life was generally preferred. Scriptural images justified this preference: Mary was the contemplative and Martha the active—and Jesus said that Mary had chosen the better part; Rachel was the contemplative and Leah the active; St. John (the Beloved Disciple) was the contemplative and St. Peter the active. In each case the contemplative was claimed to have found the better part. St. Bernard (best known of the twelfth-century Cistercians) wrote that the monk should *"always* prefer" contemplation to active involvement. And Merton quoted him often (TMSB, 39, 46, 70; CP, 52, 54; SSM, 415). The wholly active person can make no sense of contemplation, for the active person values self and others by what one has achieved, by one's success. To counter this Merton would advise: "Be anything you like, be madmen, drunks, and bastards of every shape and form, but at all costs avoid one thing: success" (L&L, 10). For Merton saw the Gospels calling us away from objective goals of success. It asks us "to prefer the apparent uselessness, the apparent unproductiveness, the apparent inactivity of simply sitting at the feet of Jesus and listening to him" (CWA, 374).

But the matter is not that simple, for contemplation itself involves an "intense activity;" it is both a passivity and an activity. If contemplation was a sleeping, it was also a waking

(TMSB, 55). Again the image of attentive listening would be the best way of understanding contemplation. In listening we find ourselves passive, though the thoughts to which we listen act within us. So in contemplation we are pure passivity as God proclaims His Word. We are passive as God acts within us. In short, contemplation is perfect action and perfect rest (SDM, 76; WTW, 97, 99).

St. Bernard claimed that the monk should always prefer contemplation and choose it, yet that is not the whole story. In going to contemplation some monks would find the Lord they meet is sending them out to action, to a ministry. But this movement from contemplation to action is not something the monk should undertake on his own—it is a charism, a gift given some contemplatives. As a gift of God it is not what the contemplative should choose (TMSB, 76). Those contemplatives who are given an active mission would lead the mixed life, contemplation and action, and this is the highest form of life. (It is evident that these texts of St. Bernard—texts that Merton studied around the time of his ordination—played a significant part in Merton coming to accept himself as writer.) Bernard would tell of "certain lights and graces" being given in prayer, and the monk would be obliged to pass them on. Should the contemplative be sent to speak of these in apostolic work, this would be "better and more necessary than the joys of contemplation." This is the "mixed" life. Christ and his mother were presented as models of the mixed life. Because of their contemplation, there was an apostolic value in their good example and their inner serenity. So the monk might be active, but the monk was to manifest a *"quies in labore"*—a stillness within the work. Contemplation is not opposed to action; rather it is only through contemplation that one is able to act as one's own self apart from the demands of the times.

In his early monastic writings Merton saw the contemplative turning to action only because of a personal charism from God. Later the movement from contemplation to action seemed to be a natural process: in contemplation "the infinitely 'fontal' (source-like) creativity of our being in Being is somehow attained, and becomes in its turn a source of action and creativity in the world around us" (FV, 115). Contemplation does not show one how to do any task in particular, rather

it should enable one to "see who it is that is acting" (L&L, 13).
Is it yourself or are others acting through you?

All our acts should proceed from an inner peace, a "deeper
ground of peace and confidence and trust." And as we act we
should be aware of it, feel it. When this peace is upset we
should "STOP! Don't push, don't be too anxious to go ahead
when peace is not present. Wait until God's time" (TMA, 72).
The contemplative life is said to be nothing other than the ability to respond to this inner call easily and simply. Contemplatives have a role in today's world; they are called "to keep alive
a little flame of peace and awareness and love in a world where
it is very difficult for it to be kept alive" (TMA, 74).

This turn from the passivity of contemplation to action is
presented well in *The New Man,* written in 1954. First the
Word of God is said to draw the monk away from compulsive
action into contemplation. Then in contemplation the monk
finds oneself entitled to what the Greek Fathers of the Church
called *"parrhesia"*—and Merton translates as "free speech"
(NM, 48). The term tells of the privilege of the citizen of a free
city-state in ancient Greece; the citizen was allowed to say
whatever was on his mind. Having the full rights of the citizen,
one could be freely and perfectly present one's self. God, in giving the Christian *parrhesia,* initiates one "into the very mystery
of creative action." This enables one to look at the world and
state what one sees. Then one is like Adam naming the animals:
one is being creative; by one's own speech something new is coming into being. So the contemplative is called to be oneself "in
the highest mystical sense"—and in finally being one's self and
saying what one sees, the contemplative can even have dialogue with God. This is *parrhesia.* There can be no dialogue
with God, if all we can do is repeat what everyone is saying.
And there can be no dialogue, if we are simply the "instrument" of God saying the words He has given us. Merton had
once said that the priest should speak only the words of Christ,
and Merton had told of God "working in us and through us,"
for we are "an instrument" of God, etc. (NMI, 22; NSC, 273–
74; see also NM, 51). But in telling of *parrhesia* Merton is telling of something significantly different: here the person is an
"instrument" of no one—one speaks with one's own voice. In
parrhesia God initiates one "into the very mystery of creative

action" (NM, 54). This is what Merton means by saying we find our freedom in God: God allows us to find our own voice and act creatively on our own. The contemplative can act "freely, simply, spontaneously."

Adam had *parrhesia;* Abraham and Job had *parrhesia,* so they spoke freely with God (NM, 54, 62). Abraham argued with God and Job disagreed with Him; in each case God and a free person were able to dialogue—there was reciprocity and mutual respect. But in order to dialogue with anyone the person must find one's own voice and say what one sees. Merton believed the scriptural account of Job shows that "God respects man's liberty" (OB, 44; Z, 124). Job, the free human being, spoke freely to God. In the Fall of 1968 while traveling in India, Merton gave a talk on prayer to some Jesuit scholastics. He told them that Job had "the guts to argue with God," and added, "this is an important element in prayer" (CS, 1978, xiii, 195). In arguing with God Job was exercising the right of free speech. He could speak freely with God because he was in "a real relationship" with him. While Job's "consolers" had no relationship with God; they were only expressing the indignation the religious "system" seemed to require. They had not found their own voice; they were only defending the "God of the manuals." They were saying only what should be said by everyone in the system, while Job spoke deeply as himself.

But in addition to speaking and naming the animals, Adam "worked" in Paradise (he was placed in the Garden "to till it and keep it"). Merton would see *Genesis* placing an emphasis on Adam's active life in Paradise (NM, 51). Thus, though Adam was fully contemplative, he was also active. By his contemplation of the created world (*theoria physika*) Adam "became aware of his *mission as a worker* in God's creation" (NM, 57; emphasis added). That is, work is not simply a result of the Fall, a curse put on the human situation because of Adam's sin. Some work is intrinsic to the ideal of the contemplative life. But the work presented here would be only as much as one's soul desired. And even one's action should be a dialogue with the natural world (NM, 53). In calling it dialogue Merton is saying that the worker must "listen" to things and not simply impose one's own will on them—much as an artist must respect ("listen to") the clay or the marble. "If our work is to become contemplative, we must be free enough from things to be able to respect them instead of merely exploiting them" (NM, 52). This "listening" to the world is also the listening of contemplation; when contemplation shapes our understanding of things, our work becomes a dialogue, a union of contemplation and action.

After Adam had dialogue with God, he was able to have dialogue with nature. Only then was Eve created and Adam could have dialogue with another human. But the fact that Adam had dialogue with God before Eve was created showed Merton that words have a function more basic than human communication. "The primary function of the word is a contemplative rather than a communicative statement of what exists" (NM, 57). Words can take us with them "into the mystery of God and into the sanctuary of Him who is Holy" (NM, 55). Words express the hidden reality of things; they are seals upon the communication of our selves with God before they are means of communication with other humans. By entering into the silence of contemplation we come to see the great mystery in words. Then when the time comes for us to speak, one speaks from the silence—one speaks in a different way. If we know contemplation in our self, our words can waken contemplation in another. Words, then, are the keys "by which we can unlock, for one another, the doors of the sanctuary and direct one another into the Holy of Holies" (NM, 57). This is the speech of the contemplative; it will enable others to enter the sanctuary too. But each must enter alone; it is not a group action to which we conform. The contemplative speaks from silence and peace, and this enables others to find their own silence and peace. Thus the contemplative shares with others what has been found. It is the ideal Merton offered to those who write, teach or preach.

The motto of the Dominicans has often been used to tell of the life that mixes action and contemplation, *"Contemplata aliis tradere"*—to give to others what one has learned in contemplation. Even during his early years in the monastery when he was having trouble with his identity as a writer, Merton had praised the "mixed life" and saw the social value of the act of contemplation—something that St. Bernard had not considered (TMSB, 62). As early as 1948 Merton would claim, "If we experience God in contemplation, we experience Him not for ourselves alone, but also for others." "Contemplative life is still imperfect without sharing, without companionship, without communion." "Contemplation like all good things demands to be shared" (SC, 174; NSC, 274).

During most of his monastic life Merton, following Cassian, spoke of the monastic ideal as "purity of heart," an ideal that Merton acknowledged had much in common with the Stoic ideal of *apatheia* (Z, 131). Coming to purity of heart was sometimes presented in Merton (and in his monastic sources) as a "return to Paradise." In Paradise one could act, but like the acts of Adam described above, one would act only as much as the heart desired and for the joy of exercising one's faculties. But as Merton became aware of the social problems of his times, he began speaking of an ideal that went beyond this return to Paradise and Purity of Heart. Attaining Paradise was no longer the final goal of the contemplative; Paradise was only the place where one could begin. For Merton the ultimate end of the spiritual life was the work of building the Kingdom of God (Z, 132). And this Kingdom can be realized only when the Will of God is done on earth as it is in Heaven. But this tells of the present world in need. It tells of an active stage and a task that is beyond the monastic ideal of purity of heart.

By achieving purity of heart one has union with God and inner peace. But this is not the end, for the contemplative sees there is a work to be done *in the world,* a work that can be done only by the contemplative, only by one who is the doer of one's own deeds. The contemplative is called to build the new creation, the restoration of all things in Christ. This is the "work of God in and through man." This work involves a final and perfect consummation of all things, a work of which no mortal mysticism is able to dream. But it is the Christian ideal. Merton saw the work of building the Kingdom of God in the Christian revelation, and he believed this made Christian contemplation different than the ideal of the Stoic or Zen master. They stopped with the tranquility or the inner enlightenment. But when Christians return to Paradise, they have become sons who now can "work with the Father to establish his Kingdom of freedom" (NM, 35). This Kingdom involved "the apocalyptic marriage between God and His creation." Merton saw this presented symbolically in the final pages of the Bible; it involves a work to be done in the world. As a worldly work it tells of a stage that is beyond what is found in the Stoic or the Buddhist tradition (Z, 132).

Today the Christian contemplative is called to meet God and in so doing discover God's will for the world here and now. God is asking for human "cooperation in shaping the course of history according to the demands of divine truth, mercy and fidelity" (SD, 8). If we open our hearts to the divine will, we can share in the great work of redemption that he asks of us:

> the work of restoring order to society, and bringing peace to the world, so that eventually man may begin to be healed of his mortal sickness, and that one day a sane society may emerge from our present confusion (FV, 66–67).

These passages that tell of God calling the contemplative to reshape the world are obviously telling of more than the quiet farm work Merton had envisioned for Adam in presenting his earlier understanding of the monastic ideal. Here it would involve the contemplative acting in the turmoil of events. Merton could develop his thoughts about active, social involvement only after he learned again of the modern world. Then he would relate the contemplative and monastic tradition with the wider current of events.

The Social Thought of a Contemplative

When Merton was a university student his primary interests were literary and cultural. Yet it was during the Great Depression and the rise of Nazi Germany, and like other students he had an on-going concern with world events. When he became Catholic, he took the social teachings of the Church seriously and had even considered working in an outreach house in Harlem. While a student at Cambridge and Columbia, he became involved with student peace movements, and considering all wars unjust, he signed the Oxford Peace Pledge, saying he would refuse to fight (SSM, 144; for ambiguities in his commitment see Mott, SMTM, 83, 89, 105). Shortly before entering the monastery Merton applied for the status of conscientious objector, but he was willing to serve in hospital work (RJ, 10). In *The Seven Storey Mountain* issues of race, poverty and war were considered with both passion and distance; for then Merton saw himself a contemplative monk far removed from the troubles of the world. He had even considered this separation integral to the monastic life. In 1949 he argued,

> . . . a contemplative community will prosper to the extent that it is what it is meant to be, and shuts out the world, and withdraws from the commotion and excitement of the active life, and gives itself entirely to penance and prayer (WS, 30).

This was Merton's basic position for the first sixteen years of his monastic life, but it would change. In 1957 he read a poem by one of his novices, Ernesto Cardenal of Nicaragua, telling of the United Fruit Company exploiting the people of Central America. And gradually Merton found an awakening interest in the world he had been ignoring; soon he was trying to read accounts of all that he had missed in his years as a monk. One biographer describes him in the early sixties: "he read furiously—poetry and politics, psychology and sociology, anthropology and environmental studies, philosophy and religion" (Furlong, 240). He read accounts of the nuclear devastation of Hiroshima and Nagaski, and he was disturbed by his new awareness of American life. He learned of the Christian roots in the code words associated with the nuclear bomb ("Papacy" and "Trinity"—while someone watching a nuclear explosion said in amazement, "Lord, I believe, help thou my unbelief"). He saw the extent of the cold war and the super-powers locked in opposition while each was refining its nuclear tools of destruction.

Merton the monk took his first public stand on social issues with a 1962 article in *Commonweal:* "Nuclear War and Christian Responsibility." Here he criticized American Catholics for passively accepting the H-bomb as a weapon of defense. He soon was inviting the Jesuit peace-activist Daniel Berrigan to speak at the monastery. He became the trusted advisor of Berrigan and advised restraint in several of Berrigan's key decisions (Labrie, 93). The two poet-priests found they had much in common. In 1963 Merton edited a collection of articles, *Breakthrough to Peace.* Here the change was complete as he criticized those who "retire into the ivory tower of private spirituality and let the world blow itself to pieces" (BP, 11). In 1964 he tried to include material on peace in a collection of his own writings, *Seeds of Destruction,* but Trappist authorities would not allow articles on peace appear in the collection. But Catholic peace activists knew where Merton stood, and a mimeographed collection of his peace writings circulated in private.

Merton read William L. Shirer's *The Rise and Fall of the Third Reich* and Gordon Zahn's *German Catholics and Hitler's Wars.* He learned that many German Catholics and even monasteries of Catholic monks had quietly accepted Nazi power without significant objection. In his own times he realized that only a few Catholic moralists were speaking out on nuclear war so he complained, "We are almost in the same position as the Catholics before the last war in Hitler's Germany" (HGL, 71). He knew many of the monks he lived with were opposed to his new-found interest and his anti-war stance; so he complained to Daniel Berrigan about the "head-in-the-ground type of monk" who is usually a "fascist" anyway (HGL, 79). Merton had come out of his monastic isolation and was sharing again in the turmoil of American life.

As racial tensions mounted in the United States, Merton read *The Autobiography of Malcolm X* and the speeches of Martin Luther King. He learned of racial discrimination even in the Christian churches. Soon he was writing articles on all such issues: "From Non-violence to Black Power," "The Hot Summer of 1967," and "Is Man a Gorilla with a Gun?" Some were edged with satire: "A Devout Meditation in Memory of Adolf Eichmann," and "Auschwitz: A Family Camp." He was determined to deal with the central moral issues that were dividing America: "Machine Gun in the Fallout Shelter," "Christian Ethics and Nuclear War," and "Vietnam—An Overwhelming Atrocity." His articles were appearing in *The Catholic Worker, Ramparts,* and *The Saturday Review.* The silent monk seemed to be speaking everywhere about everything.

Merton studied the Christian traditions of "just-war" and radical nonviolence. He began quoting pacifist texts of Origen from the third century and sermons on the love of enemies by St. Maximus from the seventh century. He was encouraged by statements of recent popes and by the Catholic pacifists who visited his hermitage. He became aware of several German Christians who because of their Christian witness were executed by the Nazis: Dietrich Bonhoeffer, Alfred Delp, Franz Jagerstatter, and Max Josef Metzger. He wrote about each and questioned the present stance of the American clergy when so few were offering moral guidance on the issues of war and racism. He believed the American churches had become so involved in American politics and finance that they were compromising their prophetic vocation. They had taken the safe road of accepting the evil that other Americans had accepted and were not proclaiming the Gospel (CAW, 343).

Many of the books Merton needed for his research were not available at the monastery, so he borrowed them from libraries in Louisville and wrote to friends asking them to send appropriate material. He wrote the introduction to a collection of Gandhi's writing on peace, and in working with the texts of Gandhi developed his own thought. Like Gandhi he called for a nonviolence that included active resistance, and like Gandhi he saw nonviolence having a power through the truth it made evident.

By 1964 Merton was saying that the monastery should not try to shut out modern life—for the "monastic community is deeply implicated, for better or for worse, in the economic, political, and social structures of the contemporary world" (SD, 7). And whether the monks intended it or not, they were, in everything they did (liturgy, study or contemplation) participating in the political events they claimed to renounce. Merton was no longer claiming that contemplation would deliver the monk from worldly concerns; rather, contemplation would make the monk especially sensitive to the urgent needs of the times (CWA, 177). The monk was to have a prophetic role; he was still to abandon the world—but "only to listen more intently to the deepest, most neglected voices from it." The mystic could no longer escape the confusion and guilt of the world through a personal quest for deliverance. "The mystic and the spiritual man who in our day remain indifferent to the problems of their fellow men . . . will suffer the same deceptions, be implicated in the same crimes" (FV, 67–68). And should one try to develop an inner life without concern for the general anguish, one would develop only an inner illusion.

Though Merton called for the monk to become involved in the events of his time, he did not believe the monk was obliged to party commitment or to adopt a particular political line. Rather, "the monk should be free of the confusions and falsities of partisan dispute. The last thing in the world I would want is a clerical or monastic movement in politics" (SD, 7). The daily conflicts and political entanglements were only the surface of history anyway. The monk (or the non-monk) would have a better understanding of the world if he were not taken up with events on the front page of the daily paper. "What did the radio say this evening? I don't know" (MJ, 58; FV, 150). Merton told of being aware of the news only when it was slightly stale and no longer the pseudo-events created daily by the media. It was better to ignore the momentary crises, for they had been invented to keep the TV viewer in a state of constant agitation.

Merton would claim he was not an enthusiastic side-taker, for he believed that when one identifies with any party or faction, one does so in opposition to people (FV, 109). Parties are abstractions and people are real. "To be consciously and willingly committed to the worldly power struggle, in politics, business and war, is to founder in darkness, confusion, and sin" (SD, 97). Those striving for holiness today should be aware of world events and come to know the inner meaning of the struggle. Then they would recognize that wars and cataclysms are only the outward projections of a hidden and spiritual battle (SD, 97). Merton would often take a spiritual/ psychological perspective: he would tell of Americans being addicted to war; we are "like an alcoholic who knows that drink will destroy him but who always has a reason for drinking. So with war." And racism here or abroad was a form of collective narcissism (L&L, 114, 132). The root of today's problems is not to be found in the streets of America; it is to be found in the troubled hearts of those who live on those streets. In such observations "peace of heart" has become more than a monastic ideal; it was the only way that a troubled nation could resolve the turmoil in its streets. The monastic ideal has become a national need.

When activists of the sixties challenged Merton to leave his hermitage and come to the cities where he might share the daily struggle, Merton told of having found "the right battleground" for himself; he saw no point in assuming an absurd activist role in which he did not believe (HGL, 501–02). He told of wanting to be "halfway between in and out of the action" (HGL, 640). Contemplatives remaining in the cloister were said to be of more value to America than contemplatives engaged directly in political protest. The monks were to "preserve their unique perspective, which solitude alone can give them, and from their vantage point they must understand the world's anguish and share it in their own way" (FV, 68).

It would seem easy enough for the contemplative monk to share in the national anguish. But could the contemplative *do* anything about the anguish other than offer suitable prayer? If the contemplative is not to engage in "partisan politics" or be a "side taker," it is hard to see how the contemplative could contribute to the events of the time. That is, unless the contemplative was—like Merton himself—a talented and famous writer. In any case Merton wanted contemplatives to be concerned with the same problems as other people, but he believed they should "try to get to the spiritual and metaphysical roots of these problems—not by analysis but by simplicity" (FV, 147). Again the contemplative must look to one's own heart. The monk has a responsibility in the face of the problems of the profane world ("nuclear war, the starvation of millions of people"); these make him aware of the seriousness of his own vocation (SCh, 214). The monk would then see that he is implicated in all that goes on in the world, but he should be "detached from these struggles over particular interests only that he might give thought to the interests of all." An involvement in the anguish of the times had become integral to the monastic quest.

Though Merton was committed to nonviolence, he did not condemn every war. He even told of preferring violent resistance to "passive acquiescence" (NA, 104). But he believed that nonviolent opposition is "per se and ideally the only really effective resistance to injustice and evil." Yet his opposition to violence was not simply practical (NVA, 233). Nonviolence "is not for power, but for truth. It is not pragmatic, but prophetic" (NA, 75). It is aimed at letting the truth become manifest.

When peace activists developed antagonistic forms of protest, Merton objected that true nonviolence should not infuriate the violent; this would only lodge those supporting the Vietnam war more deeply in their "patriotism." True nonviolence should be the beginning of a dialogue. It should involve self-sacrifice and break the pattern of mutual escalation by appealing to the intelligence and freedom of the violent. Nonviolence is a recognition of human integrity apart from all causes; it is a matter in which each one must assume a personal responsibility at every moment (FV, 27). It must give expression to a fundamental truth that will enable all people to get in touch with their common identity. It makes us aware of our own weakness, yet it has nothing in common with weakness; for it demands "a lucid reason, a profound religious faith and, above all, an uncompromising and courageous spirit of self-sacrifice" (FV, 39, 44).

Merton believed the popular press in the U.S. was unable to appreciate nonviolence, and this further assured him that the contemplative had something to offer America. He reflected on a news account of Lee Harvey Oswald that spoke of Oswald as a lone wolf with a background that "showed that he was inclined to nonviolence up to a point where his mind apparently snapped" (FV, 30; see NVA, 162). Merton saw the account as an exercise in double-think; it assumed that violence was normal and any interest in nonviolence was a sign of mental aberration. Nonviolence was so irrational that one "inclined" to it was capable of any atrocity! An inclination to nonviolence is made to sound like a fateful attraction that leads people "in a hypnotic trance to perpetrate mysterious evils." Merton found such unspoken attitudes common in the popular press. To oppose this mindless appeal he wanted those practicing nonviolence to have "a solid metaphysical and religious basis" (NA, 209). This is the grounding they could discover through contemplation. The contemplative can realize the deeper truth of humanity. This reveals a fundamental human unity and frees us from the ego identities by which we are locked in opposition. Then we would not be taken in by either side or by slogans that appeal to compulsive behavior. Apart from the power blocks that control our thought we would see the simple and loving truth that is proclaimed in the Gospel.

The best way to relate contemplation to Merton's thoughts on war, racism and violence is to consider the "metaphysical" contemplation (*theoria physika*) that was considered in chapters I and II. This contemplation would give a non-reflective knowledge of one's person in the "hidden ground of love"; there all humanity is united in the one Lord. Without knowing this contemplation, one is left only with the *cogito;* that is, an objective ego identity that leads to ego identities in conflict. Then one will seek to establish one's ego in competition with others, and all will become further estranged from the truth of one's being. One would know only self-interest and would be guided by the slogans, superstitions and popular mystiques by which "worldly" people establish themselves. Worldly people hardly remember that they are grounded in love, for they are lost in the "pseudo-events" that dominate the news. They strive to become somebody by getting their names or faces into the public eye. Then the Cartesian self—the self that knows itself as an object anyway—would finally have proof that it exists. It would be the object everyone is forced to look at. One has finally become somebody—because *Who's Who* has said so and one's face is recognized "everywhere." Publicity assures us that we have a place in the current myth—but in the process our real identity has been lost.

Those who have a place in the popular myth soon will be committed to defend the myth—for they exist only through the myth. Sometimes they are asked to sacrifice their lives so that the myth might continue. And those who kill defending the myth are regarded as "healthy." Their survivors will then need the myth so that they might explain to themselves their human loss; the myth must continue.

At one time the social myths were religious, but now they are "historical, political and pseudo-scientific" (FV, 255). Today we have the myth of "progress," of "betterment through technology," and the myth of "what-is-happening-now." Each political ideology develops a myth of its own. These draw free people into a group identity wherein they become defined, often by their opposition to another group—soon everyone is so involved that no one can stand back and see the opposing factions are mirror images of each other. Free persons have found their identity in myths, and the opposing myths give their egos meaning and value. They no longer need question themselves personally, for the common myth provides all answers. They can concern themselves only with practical problems, for the basic human problems that everyone should face have been covered over by the common myth. Without facing the real human questions, those lost in the myth will see themselves only in service of the common ideal. They will only have practical problems and soon become mechanized parts of the process. They will have a passionate commitment to the myth, "a passion for unreality," and they will become violent whenever their illusion is threatened. If they die defending the myth, they know others will praise them as heroes (FV, 224). This is the dynamism of the myth, a dynamism that enables the modern world to continue. But amidst claims and counter claims real people are dying in anguish because of the "demonic abstractions" to which people have given themselves. They are so possessed by their abstract identities that they can no longer locate themselves and a personal taste for the truth. Truth can be found only by dissociating one's self from all social illusions. But this requires solitude, silence, a facing of the existential questions, and a mortification of the appetites. But, if people will let go of the airy abstractions that sustain their egos, through contemplation they can discover their truth in the hidden ground of love.

An example could illustrate what Merton means by "myth" or "abstraction." He believed that the white racists of the South were taken up by a "quasi mystical obsession with the black demon waiting in the bushes to rape the virginal white daughters of the Old South" (FV, 140). The sentence is filled with myths—abstract ideals that sound silly when stated directly. But these "abstractions" touch emotional chords and motivate groups to violence. The words appeal to group identity and lead to group violence. Contemplation would enable the white racist to see that the "negro problem" is really the white man's problem, "rooted in the heart of the white man himself" (SD, 41; FV, 168). The white racist is possessed by abstract demons, "virginal white daughters," "the Old South," and if these demons are threatened he will use violence to de-

fend them. Merton saw America in the Vietnam war defending
the myth of the American cowboy; with a handy six-gun America would take on any troublemaker in town. Those we were
opposing were guided by another myth, a Communist world
order, and as the myths fought it out, real people were dying.
We have been told to love one another, but instead we have
loved our abstractions and killed one another. "We do not
know ourselves or our adversaries. We are myths to ourselves
and they are myths to us. We are secretly persuaded we can
shoot it out like the sheriffs and cattle rustlers on TV. This is
not reality." Merton used a phrase of St. Paul to tell of America
being captivated by the "elements and powers of the air" (Paul
to the Galatians). These airy powers were the myths that America had talked into existence. Having talked ourselves into be-
lieving in these fictions, we are pulled about by the airy powers
we have devised. We have become living victims of "the Babel
of tongues that we call mass society" (FV, 150). We can be
healed only by forgetting the buzz words that guide us and returning to silence.

Several days before he entered the monastery Merton wrote to
a friend: "It is time to stop arguing with the seven guys who
argue inside my own head" (RJ, 163). This was the Babel he
hoped to avoid. But even though the monk withdraws from the
world, he can carry all the abstract demons with him. These
might even sustain him in his monastic life, but they are the illusions that any good spiritual director should eliminate. The
"seven guys" must be silenced so that one might move beyond
the abstract debates. Then the monk can face the true human
questions. These do not concern myths in conflict, nor are
they practical questions about implementing the myth. They
are the great existential questions that the myths have concealed, the personal questions that each one must answer in
fear and trembling.

Today language has broken down; words are invoked to sustain our illusions; they serve only as emotional triggers that
render dialogue impossible. Violence arises from this general
crisis of language. So Merton called for a fundamental purification of the way we speak (NA, 74). He believed the reality of
war was covered up with double-talk so that no one knows
what is really involved. Merton tells of a U.S. major in Viet-

nam saying, "It became necessary to destroy the town in order to save it" (NA, 238). And this is accepted as significant! A "free zone" came to refer to an area in which anyone can be shot, and "pacification" of a town might involve the death of its inhabitants. Language is twisted to make us look good; verbal magic has concealed the reality. We can speak nobly of ourselves as reluctant to use force, but then we claim we must use force for the enemy understands nothing else. We have accepted our own violence by claiming it is the only way we can deal with the enemy—and the enemy is making the same claim about us. And no one wants to see what is happening. We are protected by words that show us to be innocent, and we never recognize we are caught in a web of double-talk. Since the enemy is said to lie and cheat, there is evidently no point in talking with the enemy. A jumble of nonsense has covered the situation, and words trigger our automatic response. Language can no longer reveal truth. It is only an element in the big game by which one outwits the others, and all live in a web of "self-enclosed narcissism." And as long as no one objects, no one need confront the living God. Such is the violent world in which we lead our bewildered lives. Contemplation might deliver us from this world, for contemplation would show us that it does not exist. Beyond all words in the silence of contemplation we would see our personal weakness and see that all of us are bound together in love. Then, recognizing our common unity, we would no longer need to invoke mythic powers to conceal ourselves. Language would be restored and honest words would be exchanged in dialogue.

In 1968 Merton was given permission to travel to Asia to speak in Calcutta at a gathering of monks from different faiths and in Bangkok at a gathering of Christian monks and nuns. For his address in Bangkok on December 10 he chose to speak on "Marxism and Monastic Perspectives." He had had an interest in Communism since he attended Party gatherings as a student at Columbia. Now he was telling of a recent meeting with a young French Marxist in California who startled him with the claim: "We are monks also!" Merton repeated the claim in Bangkok and went on to tell of the ideal Communist society wherein "each gives according to his capacity and each receives according to his needs." And he identified that with the monastic ideal. Both the monk and the Marxist believe that "the claims of the world are fraudulent." He acknowledged that the Communists had persecuted the monks of Tibet, but beyond the powerblocks of the cold war he wanted to tell of a common human ideal that might enable dialogue. He then went on to see Marx asking people to evolve from *cupiditas* to *caritas.* Again he was trying to see beyond evident differences (AJ, 326–43).

By his presentation he wanted to show that the monk was not apart from the social anguish of the times. Monastic life could still present an ideal of deliverance to those who had become lost in the struggle. The common life of a monastery could still serve as an ideal place of refuge apart from the evident divisions of a weary world. Merton seemed to be telling the monks and nuns that the unifying power holding the monastery together (*caritas*) was the same unifying power holding the universe together. It seemed a young French Marxist had recognized the power, the same power Merton recognized when he first visited Gethsemani years before. That is why he had called Gethsemani the "center of America."

Merton's talk in Bangkok was recorded on videotape. When he had finished he shyly waved away the cameras and said, "So I will disappear from view and we can all have a Coke or something." These are his last recorded words; he would soon be dead. He was speaking at the center of Asia, but the American life he had loved and criticized shaped the final words of the mystic who spoke to the heart of America.

Epilogue

In the summer of 1941—before entering the monastery—
Thomas Merton wrote a novel whose central character was
called Thomas Merton. This "Merton" made a visit to England and German-occupied France as Europe was enmeshed
in World War II. The novel, *My Argument with the Gestapo,* is
subtitled *A Macaronic Journal.* Macaronic refers to the jum-
bled mix of pseudo words that run through the narrative. It
suggests the meaningless propaganda uttered by opposing
sides as they developed their power blocks. People in the novel
make noble statements about why they are fighting and why
they are willing to die, but "Merton" (the central character)
says, "I have no ideas about justice, who is right, who is
wrong." He will not identify with any nation. "I am not for any
side in the War. I believe in peace."

After hearing people state their conflicting ideals "Merton"
responds, "I want to die knowing something besides double-
talk" (MAG, 76, 258, 78). The whole world was a prison, but
"Merton" knew he was free, for he was a child of God—
delivered from the conflicts of the world. He even thought of
himself as "a kind of a Trappist," who can speak to the world
only in "equivocal jokes." He tells of the world being eager for
the books that he will one day write: books that will tell of God
in a "new witty and pertinent way" and would guide the reader
through the muck of contemporary civilization. He would
write of his own life until it became clear to himself and free
from the myths of the world—though the process might take
one hundred books (MAG, 157, 188, 53).

The novel is obviously prophetic. The real Thomas Merton
would withdraw into a Trappist silence wherein he would write

an abundance of books telling of his own life and seeking to say something apart from the Babel of language. During his first years as a monk, he spoke the clichés of Catholic piety and monastic life, but then he forged a language of his own, simple and direct and filled with the American idiom. He would tell of people confused by meaningless language and, like the character in his novel, he would insist on stepping aside from causes and abstractions to speak with his own voice. In his early days in the monastery Thomas Merton found a conflict between the monk and the writer. Yet Merton's double identity (monk and writer) remained integral to the vision stated in the novel written in the summer of 1941. The writer needed a life of silence, but not to remain silent—he was silent only to be able to speak the truth that those lost in the daily noise can never speak.

Merton would often tell of a death and a resurrection, a disintegration and a new integration. He must lose his identity to find his identity; he must lose his freedom to find his freedom. He must lose his community of friends, so that he might truly be a friend; he must lose his voice, so that he might learn to speak. Many have argued that Merton was more truly a writer than a monk. But though Merton himself knew the conflict and the paradox involved, the double-identity was who he was. He was following the Gospel command to lose one's self for Christ, for then the self might be found. Like Jonah he could become a writer—only by a round-about journey in the belly of a paradox. But one is struck by the prophetic words of *My Argument with the Gestapo.* He was seeking freedom in a compulsive world, and this involved his sensitivity as a writer: "If there is a kind of freedom that can be advanced by bad writing, I don't want any part of it" (MAG, 257). He could find this freedom only within the restrictions of monastic life. He must make a radical surrender to God; then, if God wanted him to be a writer, this would be given to him as a "charism"—a gift. But for his part he must break with all the voices of the world. Thereby he could hear what the world was saying and speak to it in response.

Merton came to accept himself as both contemplative and writer. Yet the tension continued. There were times he was fed-up with his monastic community and say that among them he was not in his right mind, but there were also times he was fed-up with his writing ("I am surfeited with words and type-scripts and print" [VC, 46]). If he criticized the monks for their compulsive behavior, he could also recognize that his own writing had become compulsive. But in the end he remained very much a Trappist monk and very much a writer.

Merton often looked back to the November evening in 1941 when he made his decision to enter Gethsemani. He told of his mind being filled with the conviction that he should become a monk. He hesitated for a moment, yet sensed there could be no further delay. "I must talk to somebody who would settle it. It could be done in five minutes. And now was the time. Now" (SSM, 363). He was teaching at St. Bonaventure College and soon was hurrying about the campus looking for a priest to present some final questions. The priest gave words of reassurance and scales seemed to fall from Merton's eyes. His worries seemed empty and futile. "Yes, it was obvious that I was called to the monastic life: and all my doubts about it had been mostly shadows" (SSM, 365). He told the priest: "I want to give God everything." Many years later he reflected that his words were not premeditated and that he meant what he said (VC, 92).

The decision to enter the monastery and the prior decision for priesthood would determine the rest of his life. The two moments show a central element in the writings of Merton: decision. He made several radical decisions and each time he sensed the presence of God; after these moments his freedom could be found only in the decisions. He would continue to think of himself as "a stranger and wanderer on the earth" (VC, 43), for beyond the earth, his decisions were made before God. By his response he had defined himself. Two wills had formed his vocation.

There is another important moment of decision in Merton's life. It came when he first went to Mass in 1938. In Corpus Christi Church near Columbia University he heard a young priest tell the assembled believers that the Second Person of the Trinity had assumed a human nature; this divine Person walked among us and "died for us on the Cross, God of God, Light of Light, True God of True God" (SSM, 209). And as the priest repeated the basic elements of the Catholic faith Merton felt the full weight of the Christian tradition behind the words.

He was dazed by the words, and—not waiting for the rest of mass—hurried from the Church feeling he dwelt in the Elysian fields. Years later he would set in bold type-face the importance of such moments: The deepest truths of human nature are revealed in an event that "HAS THE NATURE OF *KAIROS,* CRISIS OR JUDGMENT." One is challenged "BY A DIRECT HISTORICAL INTERVENTION OF GOD"—an intervention that may be doubtful or obscure, but is nonetheless decisive. At the time of this intervention one is called upon to "RESPOND WITH THE ENGAGEMENT OF HIS DEEPEST FREEDOM, OR HE CAN EVADE THE ENCOUNTER BY VARIOUS SPECIOUS EXCUSES." But "IF THE ENCOUNTER IS EVADED, MAN'S FREEDOM IS NOT VINDICATED BUT IS MORTGAGED AND FORFEITED" (OB, 84). Merton believed God so encounters every human being, and the human must make a fundamental decision. This had occurred in his own life. He had heard the faith forcefully proclaimed, and in hearing it he stood free of the empty verbiage that had cluttered his mind. In this *kairos,* judgment or encounter, this "direct historical intervention of God," he had discovered a freedom apart from this world—he believed he had encountered God, so he took the first steps that would enable him to say, "I want to give God everything." He had found the spiritual courage that "dares to commit itself irrevocably" (MJ, 21).

The great events of Merton's life and every life concern the "secret and mutual exchange between the invisible spirit of man and the transcendent Spirit of God" (MJ, 84). This is the encounter that takes us beyond ourselves and makes us free; "We are most truly free in the encounter of our hearts with God in his word" (HGL, 159). But the word of God demands of one a response, "a personal engagement, a decision and commitment of his freedom, a judgment regarding an ultimate question" (OB, 71). The response is the act by which one gives everything to God—only then has one discovered who one is; then one is free and one is committed. Freedom is not apart from commitment, rather freedom is "the capacity to commit ourselves, to give ourselves, to surrender ourselves, to pay the supreme homage of our inmost being to what we have chosen as our good" (MJ, 77). Merton made such a commitment and recommended it to others:

Our encounter with God should be, at the same time, the discovery of our own deepest freedom. If we never encounter
Him, our freedom never fully develops. It develops only in the
existential encounter between the Christian and God, or between *man* and God—because not only Christians encounter God. Every man at some point in his life encounters God,
and many who are not Christians have responded to God
better than Christians. Our encounter with Him, our response to His Word is the drawing forth and calling out of
our deepest freedom, our true identity (CWA, 344).

The passage tells of Merton's own life. Through this and
other such passages Merton offers a radical challenge to the un-
committed people of America. Many of these might read his
texts for daily inspiration. But they might still avoid the radical
commitment that Merton saw necessary for freedom. Merton
spoke with an urgency as he made his monastic decision: "Now
there could be no delaying . . . now was the time. Now." It was
the *kairos,* the encounter, and Merton responded to it with an
intensity that many of us can hardly understand. But the free
intervention of God and Merton's free response made all the
difference. This sense of dedication runs through the writing of
Merton. It was the dedication that required a discipline and
that enabled him to be free.

By his monastic life Merton would tell of exploring a strange
and difficult world; he was risking "his mind in the desert beyond language and beyond ideas" where "God is encountered
in the nakedness of pure trust" (MJ, 223). Yet by dwelling in
that land he came to have a message for those troubled by their
lack of faith and unable to believe there can be such an encounter. In August 1967 Pope Paul VI asked the contemplative orders what they had to say to the modern world. When the
request was forwarded to Merton, he did not have time to consider his response. So he wrote saying he did not want to write
a solemn pronouncement that would only drive the modern
world more deeply into despair. He did not want his answer to
tell of a different world that one enters only by dint of a dedicated will. What he knew was more simple. He had discovered
he was a brother to the modern world in all of its confusion.
Yet he had something to say:

The message of hope the contemplative offers you, then, brother, is not that you need to find your way through the jungle of language and problems that surround God; but that whether you understand or not, God loves you, is present to you, lives in you, dwells in you, calls you, saves you, and offers you an understanding and light which are nothing like you ever found in books or heard in sermons. The contemplative has nothing to tell you except to reassure you and say that if you dare to penetrate your own silence and dare to advance without fear into the solitude of your own heart, and risk the sharing of that solitude with the lonely other who seeks God with you and through you, then you will truly recover the light and the capacity to understand what is beyond words and beyond explanations because it is too close to be explained; it is the intimate union in the depths of your own heart, of God's spirit and your own secret inmost self, so that you and He are in all truth One Spirit. I love you in Christ (MJ, 223).

He wrote the text in haste and the message is familiar, but to people like myself no one else could say it so well.

Bibliography

Books by Merton:

AJ   *The Asian Journal.* Edited by Naomi Burton, Brother Patrick Hart, and James Laughlin. New York: New Directions, 1973.

AT   *The Ascent to Truth.* New York: Harcourt Brace Jovanovich, 1951.

BP   *Breakthrough to Peace,* edited and with an introduction by Merton. New York: New Directions, 1962.

BW   *Bread in the Wilderness.* Collegeville: The Liturgical Press, 1971.

CGB   *Conjectures of a Guilty Bystander.* Garden City: Image Books, 1968.

CP   *Contemplative Prayer.* Garden City: Image Books, 1971.

CWA   *Contemplation in a World of Action.* Garden City: Image Books, 1973.

DQ   *Disputed Questions.* New York: Mentor Omega, 1953.

EEG   *Exile Ends in Glory.* Milwaukee: Bruce, 1948.

FA   *Figures for an Apocalypse.* New York: New Directions, 1947.

FV   *Faith and Violence.* Notre Dame: University of Notre Dame Press, 1968.

HGL   *The Hidden Ground of Love: The Letters of Thomas Merton on Religious Experience and Social Concerns.* Edited by William H. Shannon. New York: Farrar, Straus, Giroux, 1985.

HR   *Honorable Reader: Reflections on My Work.* New York: Crossroad, 1989.

L&L   *Love and Living.* Edited by Naomi Burton Stone and Brother Patrick Hart. New York: Bantam, 1980.

MAG   *My Argument with the Gestapo: A Macaronic Journal.* New York: New Directions, 1975.

MJ   *The Monastic Journey.* Edited by Brother Patrick Hart. Garden City: Image Books, 1978.

MSB   *Merton on Saint Bernard.* Cistercian Publications: Kalamazoo, 1980.

MZM   *Mystics and Zen Masters.* New York: Dell, 1969.

NA   *The Nonviolent Alternative* (revised edition of *Thomas Merton on Peace*), edited by Gordon Zahn. New York: Farrar, Straus, Giroux, 1980.

NM   *The New Man.* New York: Mentor Omega, 1963.

NMI   *No Man Is an Island.* New York: Harcourt Brace Jovanovich, 1955.

NSC   *New Seeds of Contemplation.* New York: New Directions, 1962.

OB   *Opening the Bible.* Collegeville: The Liturgical Press, 1970.

R   *A Thomas Merton Reader.* Revised edition; edited by Thomas P. McDonnell. Garden City: Image Books, 1974.

RJ   *The Road to Joy: The Letters of Thomas Merton to New and Old Friends.* Edited by Robert E. Daggy. New York: Farrar, Straus, Giroux, 1989.

RU   *Raids on the Unspeakable.* New York: New Directions, 1966.

SC   *Seeds of Contemplation.* New York: Dell, 1949.

SCb   *Seasons of Celebration.* New York: Farrar, Straus, Giroux, 1965.

SCh   *The School of Charity: The Letters of Thomas Merton on Religious Renewal and Spiritual Direction.* Edited by Brother Patrick Hart. New York: Farrar, Straus, Giroux, 1990.

SDM   *Spiritual Direction and Meditation.* Collegeville: The Liturgical Press, 1960.

ScJ   *The Secular Journal of Thomas Merton.* New York: Dell, 1960.

SJ   *The Sign of Jonas.* New York: Image Books, 1956.

SL   *The Silent Life.* New York: Farrar, Straus, Giroux, 1988.

SSM   *The Seven Storey Mountain.* New York: Harcourt Brace Jovanovich, 1948.

TMA   *Thomas Merton in Alaska, The Alaskan Conferences, Journals, and Letters.* New York: New Directions, 1988.

TS   *Thoughts in Solitude.* New York: Farrar, Straus, and Cudahy, 1958.

VC   *A Vow of Conversation, Journals 1964–1964.* Edited by Naomi Burton Stone. New York: Farrar, Straus, Giroux, 1988.

WC   *What is Contemplation?* London: Burns, Oates & Washbourne, 1950.

WCT   *The Way of Chuang Tzu.* New York: New Directions, 1969.

WD   *The Wisdom of the Desert.* New York: New Directions, 1970.

WS   *The Waters of Siloe.* New York: Image Books, 1962.

WTW   *What Are These Wounds?* Milwaukee: Bruce, 1950.

Z   *Zen and the Birds of Appetite.* New York: New Directions, 1968.

Works by Thomas Merton cited in the text and not available in his books.

"Aelred of Rievaulx and the Cistercians." *Cistercian Studies,* 1987, Vol. xxii.

"The Ascetic Life, Experience of God and Freedom." *Cistercian Studies,* 1974, vol. ix.

"The Catholic and Creativity," *The American Benedictine Review,* December 1960, vol. 11.

The City of God, by St. Augustine. Introduction by Thomas Merton. New York: Random House, 1950.

"The Dark Path," *Cistercian Studies,* 1983, vol. xviii; and 1984, vol. xix.

"*Todo y Nada*—Writing and Contemplation," *Renascence,* 1950, vol. II, no. 2.

"Towards a Theology of Prayer." *Cistercian Studies,* 1978, vol. xiii.

"Thomas Merton on Renunciation," *The Catholic World,* September 1950.

Tapes of Thomas Merton: "Contemplation and Renunciation" "Contemplation and Life," "Life and Truth," "Natural Contemplation." Credence Tapes, Kansas City: Sheed and Ward.

Books by other authors mentioned in the text.

Augustine, *The Confessions.* Translation by Rex Warner. New York: New American Library, 1963.

Bailey, Raymond, *Thomas Merton on Mysticism.* New York: Doubleday Image, 1975.

Carr, Anne E., *A Search for Wisdom & Spirit: Thomas Merton's Theology of the Self.* Notre Dame: Notre Dame University Press, 1988.

Cashen, Richard Anthony. *Solitude in the Thought of Thomas Merton.* Kalamazoo: Cistercian Publications, 1981.

Cooper, David D. *Thomas Merton's Art of Denial: The Evolution of a Radical Humanist.* Athens, Georgia: University of Georgia Press, 1989.

Furlong, Monica, *Merton: A Biography.* New York: Harper & Row, 1980.

Grayston, Donald. *Thomas Merton: The Development of a Spiritual Theologian.* Lewiston, New York: The Edwin Mellen Press, 1985.

Griffin, John Howard, *Follow the Ecstasy.* Mansfield, Texas: Latitudes Press, 1963.

Hart, Patrick (editor), *Thomas Merton; Monk.* Garden City, New York: Image Books, 1974.

Kierkegaard, Soren. *Either/Or,* Volume II. Translation by Walter Lowrie. New York: Doubleday Anchor, 1959.

King, Thomas M., *Enchantments: Religion and the Power of the Word.* Kansas City: Sheed & Ward, 1989.

King, Thomas M., *Sartre and the Sacred.* Chicago: University of Chicago Press, 1974.

Labrie, Ross, *The Writings of Daniel Berrigan.* University of America Press: Lanham, New York, 1989.

Maritain, Jacques, *Scholasticism & Politics.* New York: Macmillan, 1940.

Mott, Michael, *The Seven Mountains of Thomas Merton.* Boston: Houghton Mifflin, 1984.

Powaski, Ronald E., *Thomas Merton on Nuclear Weapons.* Chicago: Loyola University Press, 1988.

Pennington, M. Basil, *Thomas Merton, Brother Monk.* New York: Harper & Row, 1987.

Shannon, Thomas H. *Thomas Merton's Dark Path: The Inner Experience of a Contemplative.* New York: Farrar, Straus, and Giroux, 1981.

Wilkes, Paul (editor) *MERTON, by Those Who Knew Him Best.* San Francisco: Harper & Row, 1987.

Several references are to the unprinted material available in the Thomas Merton Studies Center, Bellarmine College, Louisville, Kentucky.